IS GOD REALLY GOOD?

Conversations with a Theodicist

George B. Wall

UNIVERSITY
PRESS OF
AMERICA

To

my wife, Amelia
and
my daughters, Karen and Susan

whose tolerance and good natured criticisms have pro-
duced more good in one part of the world than they will
ever know

CONTENTS

PREFACE

Although some religions have been willing to represent their god or gods as amoral, or even cruel and arbitrary, the religions of Judaism and Christianity have not been willing to represent their god as anything but good, perfectly good. Yet the world we live in is not perfectly good; it teems with evils of all sorts, evils which may strip us, like Job, of all that is dear to us, including our own health. What, then, are we to say of God's goodness? We may, of course, simply close our eyes, grit our teeth, and keep repeating, "God is good! God is good!" However, if even a grain of intellectual self-respect remains within us, our words will soon ring hollow, and we will be constrained to confront in full view the chasm between our claims about God and the facts about the world. Yes, we will be constrained further to struggle with bridging that formidable chasm, using designs and materials of less than assured merit, continually having before us the remains of previous failed attempts. Yet build we must, though all may come crashing down in the end.

Thus, in the pages of this book I have attempted to build, to bridge the chasm, to get from the world in which we live to a wholly good god, to construct a theodicy. One reason why constructing a theodicy is so difficult is that the range for creativity in design is severely limited. Only certain aspects of God's character may be treated as variables, namely, his power and knowledge--certainly not his goodness. That is fixed. Attempts to be creative with God's goodness normally end in nothing but a serious attenuation of his goodness. I have chosen to work with God's knowledge; indeed, whatever is novel in my theodicy follows from the views I take of God's knowledge, views which, I hold, do not require the abandonment of God's omniscience. My appeal to freedom is, of course, not novel, although the way I treat human freedom, the way I develop the notion of responsible freedom, does provide, I think, for a strengthening of the free-will defense. At any rate, what I offer in this book is one form of a free-will theodicy.

INTRODUCTION

The height, the depth, the breadth, the width--in short, the fearful quantity and quality of evil in the world have posed a potent threat to the goodness of God. Theists, fully cognizant of the threat, have responded with a manifold of defenses, defenses which usually appeal in one way or another to the notion of freedom. For the sake of order and simplicity I shall arrange these defenses into two general types. One type, which I shall refer to as a free-will consistency defense (or consistency defense, for short), has the very limited objective of showing that God's goodness is not necessarily inconsistent with the evil in the world; that is, the defense need come up with no more than a possible explanation of the evil in the world, an explanation in which the statements need not be either true, credible, or plausible, just possible in the sense of 'logically possible'. The other type of defense, a free-will theodicy (or theodicy, for short), attempts to come up with something more than a possible explanation. What that more is could, and probably would, be expressed in a variety of ways. I shall say that the "more" consists of this, namely, an explanation which is at least as plausible as its denial. (Since the denial would encompass every alternative explanation, an explanation as plausible as its denial is, in effect, an explanation as plausible as any of its alternatives.) But what is an explanation as plausible as its denial? What conditions must it meet?

To begin with, it must be as parsimonious as its denial. Simplicity stands as an essential requirement in all our theorizing. Apart from the requirement we could still be advocates of Ptolemaic theory or of the universal ether; indeed, we could even be members in good-standing of the Flat Earth Society. Membership in the Society would hardly require the denial of any observational data or the brazen acceptance of inconsistency. All that would be required is the "flexibility" to generate ad hoc hypotheses whenever observations did not fit the flat-earth theory.

Since the requirement of simplicity is a general requirement in our theorizing, it naturally holds both in science and philosophy, including the philosophy of religion. Why, for example, is monotheism the preferred form of religion? Hume pointedly observed that the universe could have been created by a committee of gods, wryly adding that some parts of the universe look very much like committee work. Yet theists have not gone for committee theories. Why not? One reason is surely simplicity.

Admittedly, the concept of simplicity has its vagaries. As a matter of fact, the elucidation of the concept is still at an inchoate stage. However, the lack of complete clarity in the concept no more removes the possibility of making proper judgments of simplicity than does the absence of explicit canons of logic remove the possibility of reasoning correctly. Indeed, clarifying the concept of simplicity must involve samples of proper judgments of simplicity, such as that the Copernican theory is simpler than the Ptolemaic. Put differently, clarifying the concept of simplicity requires clear-cut or paradigm cases, cases we, as a matter of fact, seem to have little trouble finding. In short, the concept of simplicity, although far from perfectly clear, is clear enough to permit unambiguous judgments in ever so many instances, including, presumably, the instance of a theodicy.

Simplicity, then, stands as a requirement for a theodicy. The consequence is that some explanations of evil will just never do. One is Alvin Plantinga's suggestion that natural evil be charged to the account of evil spirits.[1] Of course, Plantinga is not after a theodicy but what he calls a free-will defense, which is a form of a free-will consistency defense. However, assuming for the sake of argument that the appeal to evil spirits turns the charge of inconsistency, we would have to say that it does so at enormous cost. First of all, the appeal plays fast and loose with Biblical data. The idea that all natural evil, or even a major portion of it, is due to evil spirits is not an idea readily gleaned from the Bible. Worse, though, the appeal just ignores the rule of simplicity. Given that many natural evils may now be fully explained by natural causes, we have to say that appealing to evil spirits is nothing less than a blatant multiplication of entities beyond necessity, an audacious jettisoning of Occam's Razor. Once that venerable razor is jettisoned, explanatory growth becomes unrestrained. If evil spirits, then why not gremlins, elves, vital essences, whatever?

The second condition for an explanation as plausible as its denial is that its crucial statements--both normative and non-normative--be as plausible as their denials. The first question, of course, is: What is

a crucial statement? A crucial statement within an explanation constituting a theodicy will here be viewed
as a statement without which the conclusion concerning
God's total goodness would not follow; that is, if the
statement were removed and not replaced, the conclusion
that God is wholly good could not be deduced. The
structure of the explanation offered by a theodicy is
assumed by me to be deductive: The reasons for the
evil in the world function as premises of an argument
from which the conclusion--God is wholly good--may be
deduced.

The next question is: What does the phrase 'as
plausible as its denial' mean? I shall say that a
statement as plausible as its denial is one which has
as good reasons for it as for its denial. An example
of a non-normative statement of this sort is the statement that there is life after death, a statement which
is normally incorporated into a theodicy as a crucial
statement. My view is that a fair appraisal of the
argumentative battleground indicates that the sides are
at a standoff, that the reasons for affirming an afterlife are as good as the reasons for denying an afterlife. An example of a normative statement which has
as good reasons for it as for its denial is the value
judgment that a world in which persons are free and
responsible is better than any world in which persons
are not free. This judgment, or a variation of it, is
also normally incorporated into a theodicy as a crucial
statement.

Perhaps, though, I should pause here to clarify my
view of good reasons in the case of value and moral
statements. Good reasons in the case of value and moral
statements are connected, I should say, with what may
be called the conditions for rational acceptance of
value and moral statements. Naturally, I cannot go into detail, and therefore will mention only very generally the following conditions: The person considering a
value or moral statement must 1) be qualified--that is,
be of sound mind, of adequate rational capacity, and so
on; 2) have reflected carefully on the statement, its
consequences (including the consequences of acting consistently with it), and its alternatives; and 3) have
judged the statement to be as acceptable as any alternative statement and its consequences. These conditions
for rational acceptance do not eliminate the possibility
that two people meeting the conditions will end up with
conflicting value or moral statements. In short, the
conditions do not guarantee value or moral objectivity.

At any rate, the main point is that a person who has met the conditions for rational acceptance of a value or moral statement automatically has as good a reason for the statement as for its denial.

A further point is that a person framing or accepting a given theodicy must find all the crucial value and moral statements of the theodicy rationally acceptable. The fact that someone, somewhere finds the crucial value and moral statements rationally acceptable will not do. Thus, turning again to Plantinga, we find a value statement to the effect that the noble bearing of suffering is a value justifying suffering.[2] Plantinga does not, as I read him, say that he finds the statement rationally acceptable. Of course, he need not say this, for his free-will defense requires nothing more than logically possible statements. He does say that some persons, apparently justifiably, have accepted the value statement. However, a theodicy requires something more than logically possible value and moral statements, and something more than value and moral statements which are rationally acceptable to someone, somewhere. It requires that the crucial value and moral statements be rationally acceptable to any person accepting the theodicy.

An even more stringent requirement is imposed upon a Christian theodicy: The crucial value and moral statements must not only be rationally acceptable to the person accepting the theodicy, but they must include and be consistent with the fundamental value and moral statements of Christianity, statements which, if not increasing the burden of framing a theodicy, surely do nothing to lighten the burden. For the Christian, hedging on value and moral principles is particularly difficult, since the principles were given concrete form in the life of Jesus. For example, whatever else the life of Jesus was, it was definitely a life of compassion. The Gospel stories of Jesus' healing are particularly illustrative. Whenever Jesus was presented with an opportunity to heal, he healed--at least the Gospels do not record an occasion on which he refused. Moreover, his healing is not presented as simply a sign, a demonstration of power, indicating his supernatural character. The Gospels are very clear about the role of compassion in his healing. "He saw a great throng; and he had compassion on them, and healed their sick." These words from Matthew 14:14 are representative of the entire healing ministry of Jesus: It was a ministry of the compassionate relief of suffering.

Since the Christian takes Jesus as a moral ideal, he is burdened with explaining why God does not seem to act as Jesus did. Why does not God relieve suffering from natural evil as Jesus is said to have done? The Christian simply may not leave God with one sort of goodness, Jesus with another. Acquiescing in such a discrepancy would be nothing short of acquiescing in incoherency, not to mention heresy.

The last condition for an explanation as plausible as its denial is that it contain no more mystery than its denial. Some theists believe that the attempt of humans to come up with an explanation for God's ways in the world, an attempt which amounts to trying to come up with God's reasons, is sheer madness, an expression of unbridled arrogance or extreme folly. Other theists, however, believe that the attempt is perfectly sane and reasonable. Some theists of the latter sort, especially those in the Christian camp, would justify their belief by observing that man is made in the image of God. Now the notion of the imago is not necessarily a means for getting all the way to a luminous deity. For one thing, the Biblical notion of the imago is not spelled out in sufficient detail for us to know exactly how far it can or should take us. For another, we often cannot fathom the reasons of our fellow human beings; how much less, then, the reasons of God, imago or no imago! Yet we can surely surmise reasons for action; further, in the case of humans we would be surprised to learn that the actual reasons of a person do not fall somewhere within the range of surmised reasons. The same might be said in the case of God.

However, if someone claims that God's way are not our ways, his reasons not our reasons--that is, if God's transcendence is thought to make him a wholly other-- then all our statements about God are threatened. Put differently, if God's reasons cannot be surmised because God is wholly other, then the analogy between God and man has been cut, with the unhappy consequence that any talk about God reduces to nonsense. Obviously, in such a case no explanation of evil is possible, not to mention one as plausible as its denial. The general point is that insofar as one resorts to mystery, he does not resort to a strictly reasonable explanation; or in reverse, the fewer the mysteries, the more reasonable the explanation, other things being equal. Since an explanation as plausible as its denial will be as reasonable as its denial, it cannot, other things being equal, contain more mystery.

A final remark concerns the value of a theodicy as compared to a consistency defense. The question is: where will a theodicy take us that a consistency defense will not? A consistency defense will surely not take us all the way to rational belief in God's goodness. The statement that God is wholly good, along with other statements about his character and of his reasons, may be consistent with a statement summarizing all the evil in the world; yet few would be so hardy as to hold that one may believe a set of statements simply because it is consistent. Most of our daydreams are perfectly consistent, but we are not about to believe any of them. Of course, some would say that a theodicy also will not take us all the way to rational belief in God's goodness. I think the point is debatable and would be inclined to say that either believing or withholding belief is rational in the case of an explanation as plausible as its denial. However, even if belief were not rational in such a case, faith would be.

Faith, I should say, is largely concerned with living and acting. Thus, faith often views a statement as if it were true, doing so far a variety of reasons, some of which I consider legitimate. Obviously, I cannot spell out all the legitimate reasons; suffice it to say that William James spelled out some. Naturally, I do not believe that faith may view just any statement or explanation as if it were true; or, if faith does so, it is not what I should call rational.

My view is that rational faith may proceed only with statements at least as plausible as their denials. Thus, if a theodicy is successful, if it shows what it is supposed to, one may have rational faith in God's goodness. The same may not be said for a consistency defense. Of course, before one may have rational faith in God's goodness, one must have rational faith in God's reality.

NOTES

[1] Alvin Plantings, God and Other Minds (Ithaca: Cornell University Press, 1967), pp. 149-51; God, Freedom, and Evil (New York: Harper & Row, Publishers, 1974), pp. 57-59.

[2]Plantinga, God and Other Minds, pp. 119–128.

PART I: FUNDAMENTAL PRINCIPLES

Humanist: Hey, T [Theodicist], who's the friendly
    nurse? She about ate me up when I tried to get
    into your room. Jesus, you'd think I was a ter-
    rorist.

Theodicist: Yeah, I heard a little conversation out-
    side the door. . . . Her name's Bessie. A real
    charmer.

H: You bet. . . . But look at you, man! They did some
    job on your leg. What happened, anyway? So far
    I've gotten about twenty different stories.

T: I tell a different one to each person. Have to
    keep my creativity in shape, you know.

H: Yeah . . . OK. I believe in your creativity . . .
    but how about the straight story?

T: You know that old power edger I bought--remember,
    I got a super deal on it from that fellow in
    Beulah, the guy who owns the mower shop?

H: I told you, T, that character is bad news.

T: Well, I hate to ruin your theory, but I'm here be-
    cause one of my fine friends who borrowed the edg-
    er didn't use a lockwasher when he replaced a
    blade.

H: Oh Christ, you got sliced with a blade! Damn!

T: 'Damn' is right--about cut my leg off, from the
    shin down. I mean, it really looked . . . well,
    gross--as the younger set would say. My leg look-
    ed as if it were hanging by a single tendon.

H: Jesus! . . . Did they get things back together OK?

T: Yeah, everything's supposed to be all right. I was
    in surgery for six hours.

H: Good God, man, you really must have been torn up.
    . . . Where'd all this happen? You don't mean to
    tell me that you're back to managing your rent
    property?

1

T: No way! I was down at the mission. You know, they're getting the place spruced up for the dedication--you must have seen the notice in the paper. Guess I'll have to miss the affair.

H: Ironic . . . slightly ironic, I'd say.

T: Why ironic?

H: Come on, T--or maybe they've got you all doped up.

T: Just a pain shot . . . which is presently in the process of wearing off; but I'm not about to call Bessie back in. . . . No, tell me--what's so ironic about my accident?

H: You're in no shape to get in an argument with me.

T: The hell! I've been bored out of my mind all day. Darla wouldn't bring me any books. Said I needed to rest.

H: Good ol' Darla. You really call the shots around your place, don't you?

T: We both do!--What's the irony, my friend?

H: You know damn well, T. Here you are, serving your god at the mission-------probably the only religious outfit in town that does anything constructive. In fact, I'll just let you in on a little secret. I'm a regular contributor to the mission. Have been for a couple of years.

T: How'd you keep that from me? Glad to hear it, though. . . . But as you were saying . . . .

H: I was saying that here you are, God's client, doing his work, and God apparently doesn't give a damn. I mean, isn't God supposed to care about sparrows? . . . Maybe he just cares about sparrows . . . and lets humans go to the devil.

T: H, your view of God is preposterous.

H: My view, hell! We're talking about your view, T. I must say, I've never been able to figure you out. Here you are, a philosophy professor-------you guys are constantly drawing these fine distinctions ad nauseum . . . .

2

T: So . . . a lawyer has the nerve to talk to me
     about drawing fine distinctions. I see that you're
     still good for a few laughs, H.

H: No, you didn't let me finish. What I was saying
     is that you're critical to the nth degree . . .
     until you hit religion. Then it's the only-be-
     lieve syndrome . . . although I guess you could
     kick up a great sophistic cloud of dust and make
     an absoulutely worthless argument appear perfectly
     sound.

T: I rather suspect, my good friend, that you've
     never been able to figure me out because you hold
     some very strange views--naive, I should say--
     naive views of what care and love demand of God.
     You seem to think that God should act like some
     kind of cosmic grandfather.

H: T, as I said, I'm not the one making the claims
     about God's providential care extending to minu-
     tae. And no . . . I don't think for a moment that
     a benevolent deity should bail people out of all
     their troubles, especially their self-made, idi-
     otic troubles. However, I do think that a bene-
     volent deity would make some improvements down
     here--would head off some natural disasters, elim-
     inate some disease, and restrain some aberrant
     human types.

T: Well, at least you and I believe that the present
     state of the world is not as good as it might be.

H: You believe that? I thought that the defense of
     God's goodness required you to say-------you un-
     doubtedly remember the constant refrain of Dr.
     Pangloss in Candide: "This is the best of all
     possible worlds."

T: Few theists--few theistic philosophers--would
     agree with dear Dr. Pangloss.

H: What? Are you kidding? Granted that Pangloss
     comes out looking awfully silly; yet how could a
     theist require anything less than the best from
     God?

T: Perhaps we need to look at the matter a little
     more closely. . . . The principle--I'll call it
     the Pangloss Principle--the principle that this

world must be the best of all possible worlds has at least two flaws: It's incomplete . . . and it's too strong. It's incomplete because it doesn't cover an important necessary condition for creating a world. Suppose, for example, that the only worlds God could create would be hellish worlds, worlds of overwhelming disvalue. If our world would be better than the others, not quite as hellish, the Pangloss Principle would permit God to create our world. I think that most people would say that before God creates he better be able to get a world of net value.

H: I'll buy that. No problem there. . . . But how is the Pangloss Principle too strong?

T: It's too strong because it should require only that this world be as good as--not better than--any other possible world. Contemporary philosophers have come up with a principle which goes something like this: It would have been logically impossible for God to have created a better world than this one. Just to make things more manageable, just so we don't have to repeat this principle every time we want to refer to it, I suggest that we simply refer to it as P_1.

H: I swear, T, you philosophers love to symbolize. I think you're all frustrated mathematicians. . . . Only I don't see the great difference between what you call P_1 and the Pangloss Principle. As I said, though, you guys get so tied up in verbal niceties that . . . . . .

T: I make no apologies. Word-worry is sometimes essential, especially when a degree of precision is desired. Obviously, precision is not always necessary or desirable, but in the present case I think that it is.

H: I'm not convinced. Look! Whatever wording you accept--'best of all possible worlds', 'as good as any other world'--you, my friend, have a problem. The fact is that a better world is possible. For example, you Christians continually talk about heaven.

T: Yes, and Christians also continually talk about earth as a necessary preparation for heaven.

4

H: Completely unconvincing! Suppose that the hard-
      ships of earth are necessary for developing char-
      acter traits like courage, patience . . . or love.
      What's the point? How would courage and patience
      ever be called for in heaven . . . or love, for
      that matter, sacrificial love--a love which gives
      even when it gets nothing in return but abuse,
      misunderstanding, threats . . . and yes, death?
      That's the kind of love you Christians talk about,
      you know. How would it ever be called for in
      heaven? And besides, how many earthlings, includ-
      ing all the fine Christians, really take on the
      qualities appropriate for heaven? . . . No, T, the
      idea that our earthly life is a preparation for
      heaven is a weak reed on which to lean, a weak
      reed, indeed.[1]

T: Suppose that it is. Other explanations of our
      earthly sojourn are surely possible, explanations
      which neither you nor I may have heard, or which
      nobody has even thought of yet.

H: Now you're grasping for straws. Hell, I'll grant
      the possibility, the bare logical possibility---
      ----I mean, I grant that there's nothing . . .
      absurd or . . . .

T: self-contradictory . . . . . .

H: Right, self-contradictory. There's nothing self-
      contradictory about saying that a suitable ex-
      planation of our earthly existence is secreted
      away somewhere in the far reaches of some human
      mind, present or future; but neither of us, I
      hope, is about to believe in God's goodness be-
      cause of the fractional possibility of somebody,
      somewhere, someday coming up with a decent ex-
      planation of our present messed-up world. Why,
      somebody, somewhere, someday might just show that
      the story of Snow White and The Seven Dwarfs is
      historically true. . . . Look, T, what I want are
      believable reasons why God didn't create a heaven-
      ly world at the beginning of things. None of this
      far-out stuff: There could be an explanation, but
      nobody knows what it is.

T: I'm not sure I can give you what you want. No way
      can I prove God's goodness . . . beyond a reason-
      able doubt--as you lawyers would like to have it.
      In fact, I don't think I can provide you with

5

stronger reasons <u>for</u> God's goodness than <u>against</u>. About the best I <u>can</u> do is provide for what I call rational faith.

H: So what is rational faith?

T: If I try to give you the full story on rational faith, I'll never get going on my explanation for our present messed-up world, as you call it. Suffice it to say that a rational faith in God's goodness must have as its foundation at least. . . a plausible explanation for the evil in the world--an account as plausible as its denial.[2]

H: OK, fair enough. I'll settle for that kind of account.

T: Do you want the cut or full-length version?

H: Do I go to R-rated movies, or do I wait until they come to home TV?

T: All right. I'll have to back up, though. I don't especially care for P_1.

H: Oh, so you want to start fudging at the very beginning.

T: No fudging--just a revision. You ready?

H: Ready.

T: OK, here's the revised principle: It would have been logically impossible for God to have created a world which he could have known would be better than this one. I'll call this revised principle P_2.

H: Call it P_2, P_{20} . . . whatever. Obviously, what you're trying to do is pull the rabbit out of the hat by engaging in some funny business with God's knowledge. I warn you, T, that I'm on the lookout for sophistical tricks.

T: Sophistical tricks? An innocent like me? Why, in the courtroom I'd be sliced into small pieces and eaten for lunch.

H: My foot. . . . Anyway, I take it that the purpose of your new principle, P_2-------apparently you

6

want to limit God's knowledge.

T: No, I just want to stress that God can know only the knowable.

H: Beautiful. So what else is new?

T: My point is that some things are simply impossible to know--like an indeterminate future. In other words, an indeterminate future is just an unpredictable future . . . so to say that we know an indeterminate future is the same as saying that we can predict the unpredictable--a flat-out contradiction.

H: OK, I'll buy that--except that I don't buy an unpredictable future. I mean, if we can't predict, it's because of our ignorance, not because of an indeterminate world, not because the same causal conditions can yield different effects.

T: Yes, I'm well aware of your views, H. But I'm not asking you to buy indeterminism. All I want you to buy is that indeterminism is as plausible as determinism.[3]

H: Well, if doing so will keep the conversation going . . . . . .

T: Thank you, my friend . . . although I fear that you are just setting me up for one of your classic cross-examinations.

H: Oh sure, you're shaking in your boots--you with your bag of sophistical tricks.

T: My dear suspicious friend, I must again protest my innocence. I . . . .

H: T . . . on with what you were saying.

T: Patience, my good friend, patience. . . . As I was saying-------what I want to maintain is just this: The universe, at least the universe of human action, is indeterministic. As a result, God can't infallibly predict the future, our future--any more than we can. The inconsistency holds for him as well as for us.

H: Well, we agree on something. I'd remind you,

7

though, that some people never give up. You tell
them that an indeterminate future is unpredictable
--even for God--and they resort to this idea of
God's atemporality.

T: Right. Past, present, and future are somehow time-
lessly before him.

H: Yeah, "somehow." My dear ol' priest used to take
that route. He'd say-------let's see, how did he
put it? Past, present, and future . . . no,
that's not it. I thought I'd never forget his
phraseology. Kind of quaint. Let's see . . .
the divine presence . . . oh, now I remember.
The glance of God--the _present_ glance of God ex-
tends over all time.

T: That's straight out of Thomas.[4] Your priest must
have been up on his Thomistic philosophy.

H: No, he was rusty, let me assure you. He had re-
membered a few choice phrases, but that was all.
He'd refer to God's glance and then go on--Jesus,
I can still see the pained look on his face; used
to break me up--anyway, he'd go on about God's
eternity, how it encompasses all time; finally,
he'd trail off with some remarks about the truths
of revelation, mystery, faith--you know, he'd use
all those good words which do nothing but paper
over absurdity. I mean, the idea that God's present glance takes in all the future--sheer non-
sence.

T: It's an especially strange idea for anyone who
wants to stay somewhere in the vicinity of the
Biblical god. Whatever else the god of the Bible
is, he's a temporal being-------not, of course,
in the sense of having a beginning and end but in
the sense of being thoroughly immersed in time,
of experiencing succession, the before and after.
If time were not a reality experienced by God, I
don't have the faintest notion of how God could
ever act in history. The idea of an atemporal
deity interacting with a real, non-illusory temporal sphere, not to mention the idea of such a
god somehow existing in the future or the future
being encompassed in his present being-------these
ideas are hopelessly incoherent, at least to me.
I don't suppose, though, that I need to pursue the
issue any further. The notion of an atemporal god

8

has already been duly criticized by others more able than I.[5] Besides, my solution requires only that my view of God--that he can't know an indeterminate future--that my view be as plausible as its denial. Naturally, I think that the denial of my view is simply out; but no matter. My solution . . . . . .

H: You're really offering a theodicy, aren't you?

T: Solution, theodicy, whatever you will. The point is that my solution, my theodicy, hardly requires -------actually, nobody attempting a theodicy is required to demonstrate that everything is, in fact, as he suggests. All that the theodicist really has to do is give a plausible account, as plausible as any alternative.

H: At least that's all I'm asking from you. At any rate, your theodicy is, I would assume, a Christian theodicy.

T: I'd rather say that it's a theodicy within the framework of Biblical theism. But however my theodicy is to be classed, its aim is to defend the goodness of an omnipotent, omniscient, personal god that acts in a self-revealing, redemptive way in human history.

H: The standard god of Western Theism. I think I have the picture. What I'm interested in, though, is your actual defense. So far, I haven't heard much.

T: You've heard my views about God's omniscience, and you've also heard my assumption about the indeterminacy of human history. Both are important elements in my theodicy. In fact, the next element proceeds naturally from them. You see, if God can't know the future with respect to free human action, then God's creation has to be something of an experiment.

H: Experiment? So God now becomes the Great Scientist--and by way of the positive image of the scientist you expect to cast a spell over me. An innocent with respect to sophistry--that, my good friend, you are not!

T: All that I'll admit to, H, is the use of a

9

positive image. Indeed, I'll use any positive
image which comes to mind. That's fair enough,
isn't it?

H: OK, so God is conducting an experiment, a trial
and error experiment, I take it. But what's the
point of the experiment? To see how patient man
can be with an ill-designed world?

T: Now who's playing sophistic games, trying to slip
in some question-begging?

H: Not me.

T: No, of course not. . . . But if you want an answer
to your question, here it is: The point of God's
experiment is to achieve a world of responsible
freedom.

H: Come on, T, you can do better than that. You'll
have to pardon me-------really, I don't want to
be rude, but I've heard so many varieties of the
free-will defense, none of them in the least persuasive, that maybe . . . we just ought to cut the
conversation. I admit that I have time to kill,
but I abhor reruns.

T: Me too; but I don't think that you're going to get
a rerun. Just the idea of the world as an experiment with freedom--just this idea substantially
alters the free-will defense. Of course, if you
wish to cut out . . . .

H: Well . . . maybe I'll take my chances. As I said,
I do have time to kill. . . . Carry on.

T: First of all, I need to let you know exactly where
I stand on freedom. My view is that a world in
which persons are free and employ their freedom
responsibly is better than any world in which persons are not free. I don't claim that this value
judgment is indisputable, only that it's fully as
plausible as its denial.

H: Your value judgment leaves you squarely in the
middle of the traditional camp. Nothing new in
your approach so far.

T: Oh, I don't try to jettison everything traditional.
My object is not just to be an iconoclast, you

know. All I claim is that I've introduced some modifications which significantly alter and greatly strengthen the free-will defense. For example, my defense doesn't require me to say that this world has been at least as good as any other world with less freedom. As a matter of fact, since freedom has been badly abused in this world, some world with less freedom . . . .

H: like a heavenly world, right? At least I can't conceive of heaven apart from severe restrictions on freedom.

T: Neither can I. The people of heaven definitely don't have the freedom to violate God's law. The Biblical view is that they don't violate God's law because they have a new heart--they cannot will to disobey God. Obviously, then, they're not as free as we are now. If anybody in heaven should ever happen to do something which could harm another, the action would have to be unintentional. In such a case God would intervene to prevent the harm.

H: Now, by God, you're talking benevolence! And what I want to know is: Why doesn't God shift to a heaven? Since his experiment is going badly . . . .

T: My dear H, the question is not whether God's experiment is going badly but whether God's experiment should be aborted. God is certainly not justified in letting a bad experiment run indefinitely, yet neither is he justified in calling it off prematurely. He should call it off only when he determines that the prospects for achieveing responsible freedom are dim--his experiment is unlikely to succeed.

H: The prospects look mighty dim to me. At any rate -------say, tell me, T, how can God determine anything about the prospects of freedom? I thought that an indeterminate future couldn't be known?

T: I'll tell you how God can determine the prospects of freedom the minute you tell me how you determined that the prospects look "mighty dim" . . . unless, of course, you were assuming determinism, in which case you were assuming what you weren't supposed to.

11

H: Well, ah . . . .

T: Actually, H, to deny foreknowledge of indetermi-
      nate events is not to deny all rational projection.

H: I knew it! I knew it! You philosophers just
      can't stay away from that enchanting drug, sophis-
      try. First you say that God can't know an inde-
      terminate future, but then under the rubric 'ra-
      tional projection', you smuggle God's foreknow-
      ledge back in. You expect the rubric to work as
      a general soporific . . . but I'm afraid, my
      friend, that it won't in my case.

T: Soporific? Sophistry? Nonsense! All I said is
      that God can make rational projections of indeter-
      minate events. Nothing wily . . . or novel about
      that claim. A number of scientists hold to in-
      determinism on the subatomic level; indeed, some
      maintain that indeterminism extends to the macro-
      scopic level, the world of ordinary perceptual
      objects.6 Yet none holds that preceding condi-
      tions make no difference whatsoever; for example,
      that electrons shot through diffraction slits can
      reverse course and come back through the slits .
      . . or turn into elephants. Moreover, the inde-
      terminist, as well as the determinist, believes
      in the predictability of, say, radioactive decay
      --he is not in the least reluctant to talk about
      the half-life of an element. In other words, he
      believes that he can make statistical projections
      . . . . So you see, I wasn't being even slightly
      sophistic when I said that God, although not know-
      ing the future, can make rational projections.
      Of course, I'd go on to say that God's ability to
      make projections far outstrips ours.

H: Why, of course. Now you're going to give God's
      foreknowledge back to him . . . or you're going
      to surround him with a giant cloud of mystery,
      for I seriously doubt that you can ever explain
      the superior ability of God to make projections.

T: I'll not claim that I can avoid all mystery, but
      then I don't think that anybody can. However, I
      do think that God's superior ability at project-
      ing the future can at least be made a little more
      understandable. To begin with, for example, we
      can point out that God has a more comprehensive
      grasp--I'd say complete grasp--of the present and

past.

H: You're simply going from one mystery to another--not much of a way to dispel mystery.

T: I haven't finished yet. Hear me out. You see, several courses may be taken toward explaining God's comprehensive grasp of the present and past. For example, we might say that God has universal clairvoyance and telepathy.

H: Just two more mysteries.

T: Yes, the how of clairvoyance and telepathy is far from clear.

H: Not just the how . . . but also the whether.

T: Agreed. The evidence for telepathy and clairvoyance is far from definitive . . . but not totally worthless, I'd say. The point I want to make is that if humans have the capacities of telepathy and clairvoyance, then attributing the capacities to God in a higher degree would be a reasonable procedure. Doing so would not dispel all mystery, but it would dispel some. Naturally, I'd also assume that God has extraordinary powers of analysis, integration, and inference.

H: Fine . . . but now that you have God able to make extraordinary projections, your hallowed statement--P_2 you called it--P_2 will be of little help to you. God may not have been able to <u>know</u> that his experiment would be a bust, but . . . .

T: I'm still not willing to admit that God's experiment is a bust; yet even if it is, I surely won't admit that God, given what he had to go on in the beginning, could have predicted that his experiment was very likely to be a bust. Besides, even if there had been a good likelihood of the experiment's turning out badly, God still might have risked it. He might have done so because of the high value he places on freedom.

H: Say, now that I think of it-------no, instead of saying that God could have projected how badly his experiment would go, I'm going to reverse course and say just the opposite. At the beginning, when God created man, he didn't have anything to go on;

13

he couldn't project at all. So why did he risk a bad world? Remember, you said that God shouldn't create unless he can get a world of net value.

T: Ah, the wounds of a friend. I think I prefer the flattery of my enemies. I fear that I have sustained a mortal blow.

H: From which, with your sophistic maneuvering, you will undoubtedly recover forthwith--as you always do.

T: Only by divine assistance, my good friend. In the present case, though . . . . . .

H: Get serious, T.

T: You will not even give me time to set up for my sophistic maneuver. . . . But if you must have a reply, I suppose-------I guess the first thing to do is to clarify my principle, what I'll call my net-value principle. I wouldn't want the principle to say that God may not create unless he can get a world of net value. I don't remember exactly what I said--maybe I said that; however, what I want to say, what I want my principle to state, is this: God may not create a world which he knows will not be a world of net-value.

H: So, the mortal blow turns out to be benign.

T: I _am_ feeling better, yet I still have a little way to go; I still have some things I can and need to say. First of all, I suppose I could just maintain that God did have something to go on in the beginning.

H: Oh, so you want to claim that God created other worlds before this one. Not a very good move. Since you have not even a smidgen of evidence for such worlds, your resort to them is not exactly parsimonious.

T: Yes, you're essentially correct about that. . . . However, I wasn't necessarily referring to other worlds. What I meant was that God wasn't totally in the dark. Remember, he created man and thus knew man's nature thoroughly. He'd given man the capacity to reason . . . and set up the conditions of life so that irresponsible decisions would have unhappy consequences. . . . Besides,

14

even if God didn't have anything to go on, he set boundaries on his experiment, made man both mortal and limited in power--no more satans, anyway.

H: Now you're assuming other worlds again.

T: Oh, my apologies. Actually, I was speaking symbolically. At any rate, what I _will_ assume is that God had plans to call off his experiment any time it showed signs of getting out of hand. . . . You see, basically, _you_, H, have a problem, not me.

H: _I_ have a problem? You're out of your mind.

T: No, _you_ have a problem. You can make a case against God only if you can show that he took an unwarranted risk. But you can show that he took an unwarranted risk only if you can show either that the chance of getting responsible freedom was slight to non-existent, or that God had no way of limiting his experiment . . . or that the value of a world of responsible freedom is not great enough to balance out the disvalue of a world of irresponsible freedom.

H: No way that the value of a world of responsible freedom can balance out the disvalue of a world of irresponsible freedom . . . unless you have some sort of odd notion of balancing out.

T: Nothing odd about my notion. Supposing that value could be quantified, I'd say that one unit of value balances out or equalizes one unit of disvalue; that two units of value and one of disvalue gives a net favorable balance for value of one unit; and so forth.

H: I'd say that disvalue outweighs value, so that any system of equal units . . . . . .

T: I was just trying to clarify what I had in mind. Obviously, the whole idea of a value unit is out. The fact, though, is that we constantly compare or weigh value, saying that this value offsets or balances out that disvalue. If a friend hits me up for a couple of hundred bucks but fails to pay me back, I'm not going to break off the friendship for the money: The value of continuing the friendship more than offsets the disvalue of losing the money.

15

H: OK, I get the point. I just don't agree that the value of a world of responsible freedom balances out the disvalue of a world in which freedom goes bad.

T: Maybe the reason is that you value a world of responsible freedom far less than I do.

H: Yes, and maybe you're forgetting how bad a world of freedom gone awry can be. Remember, freedom is not being abused as badly as it might be.

T: I grant that. But perhaps God will not permit freedom to run the full limit of abuse--for example, he may not be willing to let humans destroy themselves. Be that as it may, all I want to insist on now is that my value judgment is equally as plausible as yours.

H: I'll bet that I could find more people that agree with me than with you.

T: Counting noses is hardly the way to determine plausibility. Moreover, I'd just remind you, my good friend, of your view about moral and value judgments.

H: What about my view?

T: You deny that moral and value judgments are objective--that any set of moral or value judgments has universal validity.

H: What of it? . . . Oh, I see what you're going to say.

T: Right. If objectivity can't be had in the case of value judgments, then you can reject my judgment or say that you don't like it, but there's no way you can show it to be incorrect or invalid. As long as I've thought my judgment through carefully, it will go as well as yours. Granted?

H: Well . . . . . .

T: What's more, if you can't knock down my value judgment, then your case against God--saying that he took an unwarranted risk in creating this world--your case just evaporates.

H: OK, let's suppose--just for the sake of argument--
let's suppose that I can't fault God for creating
this world, for starting his experiment. What I'll
fault him for, though, is not calling off his experiment.

T: I told you earlier, H, that God should call off his
experiment only when he sees that it is unlikely to
succeed. The verdict on his experiment, however,
may very well still be out. You certainly haven't
forgotten the high hopes for inevitable progress
which so dominated the intellectual community during the latter part of the 19th and the beginning
of the 20th century. Actually, even today we do
not lack for utopians.

H: The fuzzy-minded, like the poor, will always be
with us. I expect better things of God.

T: Possibly God perceives distinct signs that the
prospects of his experiment are looking up; or perhaps he doesn't have enough to go on yet to say
anything definite about the prospects . . . or perhaps he does have enough to go on but still will
not call off his experiment immediately.

H: Now you've dug a real hole for yourself. If the
verdict is in for God, what's his problem? What
possible reason could he have for waiting?

T: A high respect for us as rational beings. You see,
my good friend, if God is really good, then he will
take into account that we as rational beings cannot
be satisfied with a decision which is simply imposed on us, one which we are peremptorily told is
correct but can't figure out for ourselves. Would
you be satisfied with such a decision?

H: Not in the least, but I can't see why God couldn't
reveal to us the basis of his decision.

T: It is entirely possible, H, that God's projection
of the future is so complicated that he simply cannot share the how of it with us. We would never
get it.

H: Unlikely, highly unlikely!

T: Well, I can't really say. At any rate, even if
you're correct, I'll just retreat to my backup

position: Maybe God is still too uncertain about the outcome of his experiment to call it off . . . or maybe things are turning around.

H: Christ, T! "Turning around"--don't be ridiculous. As for projecting the future, please tell me how certain God has to be.

T: Well, I'm surely not going to give you some sort of quantified probability figure.

H: Who said I wanted one? You're going after windmills.

T: All right, then, the question is: When, under what conditions, could God be fairly certain that freedom would not become responsible? The question is really similar to one we ask ourselves all the time. Take the alcoholic, for example. We put him in every program in existence--counseling, rehab hospitals, AA, religion, you name it--but nothing works. So what do we say? He's a hopeless case. We've given him our best shots, but we . . . .

H: You say that God has given us his best shots? I'd be more inclined to say that he's been dumping on us.

T: Well, we have a slight difference of opinion, then, don't we? . . . Oh, hello, TB [True Believer]. Glad to see you.

TB: Well, looks to me as if you and I won't be playing racquetball today.

T: Give me a couple of days.

TB: How're things going, H?

H: Not bad. . . . Long time no see.

TB: Yeah, it's been a while.

H: What happened, you drop out of Rotary?

TB: About two months ago. Got snowed under. . . . But what about you, T? I heard that you just about lost part of your leg.

T: Well, I guess it was touch and go to begin with,

but they tell me that they got the parts pasted together pretty well . . . although the surgeon tells me that I'll probably limp into the afterlife. But who believes surgeons?

H: Or in the afterlife?

TB: Same old H, I see. He must be providing you with a bunch of comfort, T.

T: Comfort . . ? No. But he has been saving me from boredom. We've been having a rather lively discussion.

TB: About what, may I ask?

T: About the theodicy I dreamed up. You and I never got very far on that.

H: Yeah, TB probably had to race off to sell another policy. You always amaze me, TB. You're supposed to be laying up treasure in heaven, yet you're shagging after the big bucks more than just about anybody I know.

TB: I don't think you're anyone to criticize my lifestyle, H . . . and no, I didn't have to race off and sell a policy. T and I got stuck on the issue of God's omniscience.

H: Really? That's probably about the only issue T and I agree on.

TB: Which means that neither of you believes in God's omniscience.

H: Well naturally, since I don't believe in God, I don't believe in his omniscience. However, what T and I agree on is that an omniscient god couldn't know everything--like the outcome of indeterminate events.

TB: An omniscient god has to know everything; otherwise he just isn't omniscient.

T: Surely, TB, you don't want to say that God can know the unknowable, any more than you would want to say that God can do the undoable.

TB: I say that nothing is undoable or unknowable for

19

God.

H: You mean to tell me that God can snuff out his own
      existence or make the past deoccur?

TB: Don't be ridiculous, H.

H: Who's being ridiculous? Have I mentioned some un-
      doable things or haven't I?

TB: Uh . . . .

H: And some things are unknowable--like knowing what
      the outcome of an indeterminate event will be.

TB: That I don't admit. Not at all.

H: But to say that some event is indeterminate is just
      to say that its outcome cannot be known until it
      occurs.

TB: On the contrary, it's only to say that the outcome
      can't be predicted infallibly.

H: Please inform us, then, how the outcome can be
      known; and you better not say that God can know
      the future because he's timeless. The Christian
      god is anything but a timeless, atemporal being--
      I mean, the god is constantly intervening in his-
      tory.

TB: Well, you've gotten one thing right about God,
      anyway.

T: Indeed he has. So what's your answer to his ques-
      tion? Since a temporal god exists now, not in the
      future, how can he know the future?

H: The trouble with you two is that you want to put
      God in a box, eliminate all mystery from him--as
      if our puny little minds could comprehend the in-
      finite God. Why, the very idea of trying to fig-
      ure out God is--well, just plainly preposterous.
      Here we are, like lost lightning bugs--erratic pin-
      pricks of light, flashing momentarily in the vast
      expanse of eternity. Just what gives us the idea
      that we're up to comprehending God? Absurd, sim-
      ply absurd! Our proper posture as mere creatures
      is that of awe, praise, wonder, and worship, not
      arrogant questioning.

H: Get off the damned preaching, TB. Jesus Christ,
     the next thing you know you'll want us to make
     some sort of "decision."

TB: Making the kind of decision you sarcastically refer
     to wouldn't harm <u>you</u> in the least.

T: All right, TB, now look. I agree with you that
     mystery surrounds God and his activity . . . and
     probably will continue to do so. But we can't
     just resort to mystery every time we get into trou-
     ble. You've got to admit that some of the diffi-
     culties we get into when we talk about God are
     strictly of our own making. Surely you don't want
     to cry mystery for every bit of nonsense that en-
     ters the religious mind. That's sheer coverup.
     The problem is: How do you determine that some
     mystery is not just the result of botched thinking
     or insufficient investigation?

TB: I think that some questions--some questions simply
     have to be left alone.

H: Hell, I give up!

T: I'll just remind you, TB, that two can play at your
     mystery game. If you appeal to mystery, so can
     anybody else, whether he be a non-theist, a Hindu,
     a satan worshipper, whatever. . . . I've got a lit-
     tle principle which I introduce to my students each
     semester . . . . . .

H: What is it, P_{200}?

T: No, I simply call it T's Principle, after a very
     distinguished personage.

H: How could I have failed to guess? . . . So how does
     it go?

T: It goes like this: What's sauce for the goose . .
     . . . . .

H: is sauce for the gander. A most profound and tech-
     nical principle. . . . But then, I realize that
     open admissions haven't done much for the quality
     of the students at the university.

T: You can say that again. Anyway, my little princi-
     ple does get at something extremely important--

fairness . . . or perhaps I should say, equal rights in reasoning. You see, TB, H and I can make whatever move you do--to say otherwise is to fall into sheer arbitrariness, an outrageous form of non-reason. So, if you appeal to mystery, we can too. . . . Yet for now, let me turn . . . .

TB: I still say that we can press questions about God too far. There comes a time when we just have to call a halt to the questioning; we just . . . .

T: Yes, but we can't just call a halt any and every time we get into trouble. As I said, the trouble may very well be of our own making, or it may be a consequence of not having taken our investigations far enough. Let me put it this way, TB: In a rational system mystery is a flaw--particularly mystery which stands as unresolvable paradox. What I mean is that there is mystery--and then there is mystery. Atomic theory is something of a mystery now. Just look at quark theory.

TB: Can't say that I know anything about the theory.

T: I don't know much myself. About all I know is that it's the "in" theory in atomic physics today. My point about the theory is that it was supposed to simplify the menagerie of sub-atomic particles --and I guess it does. Yet the theory becomes more complicated every day . . . as if . . . as if maybe we'll soon have to strike off down an altogether different path. But we don't for a moment believe that we're at a dead-end, that further inquiry will fail to penetrate the mystery of the atom. Not so with the mysteries of faith. Who in the church believes that the mystery of the Trinity . . . or of the incarnation will yield to further inquiry? Most Christians would probably agree with the Danish theologian Soren Kierkegaard on the incarnation: It's the supreme paradox--although I guess it's really no more "supreme" than the paradox of the Trinity. At any rate, I don't find theologians claiming that further investigation will resolve the paradox of the incarnation. Apparently they realize that anyone who is fully human cannot at the same time be "God of very god," and vice versa. No new piece of information is going to alter or resolve the paradox, so we're just

22

stuck with it. . . . Now don't mistake me to be
saying that some system--some comprehensive system
of belief--succeeds in eliminating all mystery of
every sort. Not at all. The best we can do-----
--Plato put it about as well as anybody: "Enough,
if we adduce probabilities as likely as any others;
for . . . we are only mortal men."7 As I said,
then, no comprehensive system avoids all mystery.
Yet the system with the fewest mysteries has to be
the best system, other things being equal. What
I mean is that mystery is a wart on any rational
system; as a consequence, eliminating or reducing
mystery stands as a constant goal. The alternative is simply to jettison any pretense of ra-
tionality--let the absurdities flow.

H: Yeah, sort of like the White Queen: She sometimes
succeeded in believing as many as six impossible
things before breakfast.8 No telling how many TB
could believe!

TB: H, you are becoming a real pain. If you . . . .
. . .

T: If we may stick to the issue-------OK?

H: Sure, fine. Fine with me.

TB: Muzzling your good friend here is likely to be the
only way that we'll ever stay on the issue.

T: Well, maybe there could be a little muzzling on
both sides. . . . What I wanted to say-------given
what I've said about mystery, you'll have to ad-
mit--both of you--that my theodicy is an improve-
ment over traditional or orthodox theodicies in at
least one point, namely, this: However much my
defense of God's goodness fails in other respects,
it is at least free of one mystery that encumbers
traditional defenses---divine foreknowledge.

H: The fundamental mystery remains, though, T--why
God doesn't do more than he's doing to reduce
suffering.

T: I'll get to that in a minute, H, but I haven't
finished with TB yet. I wanted to draw out some
consequences of his view of omniscience. . . .
First of all, TB, your view that God knows the
future without qualification obliges you to show

23

me how everything now happening will actually realize responsible freedom. Or to be more exact, what you have to show is that everything God is doing will in fact strengthen responsible freedom at least as much as anything else that could be done. My view-------I just admit that God might try some things which, as a matter of fact, don't work.

TB: Absurd, just absurd!

H: Don't get carried away, TB. Your view of omniscience is hardly less absurd than T's view that God might make a mistake or two.

T: I'm not sure I'd be happy with the word 'mistake'.

H: I didn't think you would be . . . but before you get off into your sophistic word maneuvres-------TB, I just want to ask you something: Since God can foresee everything, why didn't he create only those persons whom he foresaw would act responsibly?

T: Good question, H. What do you say, TB?

TB: No problem. I simply say that people can be shaped to live responsibly only under the conditions of evil in our present world.

H: My God! The same old threadbare theory: Evil is necessary for good. Rot! Even if the theory were true, how much evil must we have? The present world seems to be operating on the principle that if one dose of medicine is good, then taking the whole bottle is the very best. Talk about absurdity! Anyway, TB, the fact is that ever so many people go through their early life barely brushing against suffering, wickedness, and tragedy. Yet they turn out to be very responsible.

TB: Obviously, there will be exceptions to the general rule, but the exceptions only--well, what else can I say? They just prove the rule. Besides, I'm not about to say that God's sole objective in the world is to get responsible freedom. I think that God has other objectives, many of which are likely to remain hidden from our view, as in the case of Job.

H: More mysteries again. I swear, TB, you're hell-
      bent on going after mysteries.

T: I surely wouldn't deny other purposes for God, TB.
      I just haven't heard of any--or of a combination
      of any--which will even come close to accounting
      for the evil in the world. . . . However this may
      be, I want to come back to what you were saying.
      You were saying, there are exceptions to the rule
      that evil is necessary for the development of res-
      ponsible freedom. As a result, H's question, or
      a modification of it, still stands: Why didn't
      God create only those persons whom he foresaw
      would be responsible without having to experience
      evil?

TB: Maybe God didn't forsee anybody acting fully res-
      ponsibly. What I mean is that we could take a
      kind of Calvinistic view: Every free being cre-
      ated turns out to have a sort of natural depravity.
      In other words, God foresees that everybody, as a
      matter of fact, fails to be responsible in some
      respect.[9]

H: Your suggestion is irrelevant, TB. God's experi-
      ment doesn't require perfect people--at least ac-
      cording to T. The experiment would be a resound-
      ing success if people were just generally respon-
      sible. There've been plenty of people like that.
      Besides, since you hold that God is omnipotent---
      ----why didn't your omnipotent God create free
      people so that they would always choose respon-
      sibly?

TB: Simple! He wouldn't have created free people.

T: You're absolutely correct, TB. But now look at
      what you've said. You've said that God can't do
      something because to say that he could would be
      flatly inconsistent--exactly the course I've taken
      with omniscience. I fail to see, then, why you've
      been so resistant to my ideas about God's omnis-
      cience.

H: Personally, I fail to see why God couldn't create
      free people who would always choose responsibly.

TB: The point is elementary: Nobody is free if his
      actions are caused by God.

H: Who said anything about actions being caused by God? All I'm saying is that God could create people with a given physical and mental makeup such that they would always exercise their freedom responsibly. For example, why couldn't God create someone who has desires and beliefs such that he would always act humanely--say, whenever he found out that someone was a theist, he'd pity him?[10]

TB: Very funny, H.

T: H, I'm afraid that you're slipping in a form of determinism under the label of freedom. God can't create a free person in such a way that the person is guaranteed to decide or behave in a certain way. You see, any time God creates someone with a mental or physical makeup-------any time God gives someone a set of characteristics which serves as the sufficient condition for a given action, then you just don't have free action, by definition! What you've got is determinism. You simply can't have God creating a person so that he is programmed to . . . .

H: Programmed! Nice play to the galleries, T.

T: No play to the galleries, my good friend. You used the term 'mental makeup', as I remember, including under that term both beliefs and desires. Moreover your example of mental makeup was of a specific belief and a specific desire: Whenever a person believed that someone was a theist, his desire would be to . . . .

TB: pity him. How immensely humane.

H: TB, you don't even begin to grasp the depths of <u>my</u> humaneness, particularly . . . .

T: All right . . . let's keep on the topic. H . . . the point I'm making is this: If God created people with capacities which had to be exercised in a given way--that is, the capacities would be the sufficient condition for acting in a given way--or if God created people with desires which, in conjunction with a certain belief or beliefs, were the sufficient condition for bringing about a given type of action, then-------God simply wouldn't have created a free person. Labeling such a person

'free' would be like labeling black 'white'. Of
course, if you wish to say only that a person may
happen to act in a consistently responsible manner
(nothing in his physical or mental makeup guaran-
tees responsible decision making; he just happens
to thread his way through the decision thicket in
a totally responsible way), if that's what you
wish to say, then I have no objections. Naturally,
God should foresee these people who happen to act
responsibly . . . or if nobody acts completely responsibly, God should foresee those who act responsibly for the most part; that is, God should foresee them on TB's view of omniscience. So, TB,
we're back to you.

H: I say we've been on TB's case long enough--without
    effect, and without hope of effect.

TB: Now wait a minute, H.

H: Remember, TB, this conversation was originally
    between me and T, but so far I've not been able to
    get off any of my main objections to his theodicy
    --thanks to you. So T, I want to get back to you
    --actually to you and your mysteries. Let me be
    specific. So far your solution, your theodicy,
    has done little, if anything, to dispel the mys-
    tery of God's ways in the present universe. God
    seems to be off hiding somewhere. If he has a
    policy, it's a policy of non-action, a kind of
    complete hands-off policy. The problem for you
    is: We'd never think of following such a policy.
    When people abuse their freedom, we have no hesi-
    tation in restricting them. A policeman who re-
    frained from arresting a rapist on the ground that
    he didn't want to restrict the rapist's freedom
    would be booted off the force immediately. In the
    same way, an MD would be banned from medicine in
    a moment if he refrained from treating a patient
    on the ground that the patient would be morally
    benefited by suffering. Yet look at God! He does
    very little--nothing, I'd say--to restrict gross
    abuses of freedom, like the Holocaust, or devasta-
    ting diseases, like the plagues of the fifteenth
    century. Damn, those plagues just decimated the
    population of Europe. Yet where was God? Your
    guess is as good as mine--off twiddling his thumbs
    somewhere, I suppose.

T: All right, H, you've come in with your heavy

27

artillery. Of course, I believe that I have suitable answering fire, but before I let loose, let's
agree on something. I think that we can proceed
a little more systematically if we'll focus on one
part of the problem at a time. I suggest that we
deal with moral evil first and then move on to
natural evil.[11] How's that sound?

H: Fine with me.

T: How about you, TB?

TB: No problem. Proceed.

H: Uh-oh!

Bessie: It . . is . . five . . minutes . . after . .
         nine. We do have rules here, gentlemen.

H: Yeah . . . they ought to have rules against cer-
      tain types of nurses.

Bessie: What did you say?

H: I was saying that the nurses here are really pleas-
      ant. No wonder the patients heal so rapidly.

Bessie: We do what we're supposed to. As I said, we
         have rules.

H: OK, we're leaving. Jesus, I wouldn't want to get
      put in solitary. . . . I'll probably drop by again
      tomorrow, T.

T: How about coming in the afternoon . . . or will
      you be in court? We just got started.

H: I'm scheduled for court, but I may be able to make
      it. I'll get here in the evening, anyway.

TB: I'll probably see you on Tuesday, T. Have to go
      out of town tomorrow.

H: Damn, it's raining like hell outside . . . and me
      without my umbrella.

TB: I brought mine. I think we both can get a piece
      of it. . . . See you, T.

H: So long, good buddy. . . . . . Night, Bessie.

Keep up that good attitude. One of the rules, you know.

NOTES

[1] For a look at some of the difficulties posed for the goodness of God by the notion of heaven, see my article, "Heaven and a Wholly Good God," The Personalist, 58 (1977), 352-57.

[2] An account as plausible as its denial is of the same general epistemic type as what Chisholm calls a counterbalanced proposition. "A proposition is counterbalanced if there is as much, or as little, to be said in favor of accepting it as there is to be said in favor of accepting its negation." Roderick Chisholm, Theory of Knowledge, 2nd ed. (Englewood Cliffs: Prentice-Hall, 1977), footnote 6, p. 10.

[3] Determinism may be stated as follows: Every event is such that statements describing it are deducible from some set of true statements of antecedent conditions and causal laws. The correlative statement of indeterminism would be: It is not the case that every event is such that . . . and so forth. The view of determinism and indeterminism taken here essentially follows that of Bernard Berofsky. See Berofsky, Determinism (Princeton: Princeton University Press, 1971), pp. 268-69. Robert Ackermann suggests "as a logical possibility that there are real processes whose development may contain logically unanticipated states" within a deterministic framework. The suggestion is based on the unsolvability of the general halting problem for Turing Machines. See "An Alternative Free Will Defence" in Rel. Stud., 18 (1982), 370-72. If Ackermann's suggestion goes, my theodicy might work within a deterministic framework, depending on whether the limitations on God's ability to project the future would be great enough to serve the purposes of the theodicy.

[4] Thomas Aquinas, Summa Theologica, First Part, Question 14, Article 9.

[5] See, for example, Terence Penelhum, Religion and Rationality (New York: Random House, 1971), pp. 151-54 and chap. 21; Nelson Pike, "Divine Omniscience and Voluntary Action," Phil. Rev., 74 (1965), 27-46, and God and Timelessness (London: Schocken, 1970); George Schlesinger, Religion and Scientific Method (Dordrecht: Reidel, 1977), pp. 112-13.

[6] See Alfred Landé, From Dualism to Unity in Quantum Physics

(Cambridge: At the University Press, 1960), pp. 5-6.

[7] Plato, Timaeus, trans. Benjamin Jowett, in Great Books of the Western World, ed. Robert Maynard Hutchins, Vol. 7 (Chicago: Encyclopedia Britannica, Inc., 1952), p. 447b.

[8] Lewis Carroll, The Annotated Alice (New York: Bramhall House, 1960), p. 251.

[9] See Alvin Plantinga's transworld depravity defence in God, Freedom, and Evil (New York: Harper & Row Publishers, 1974), pp. 45-49.

[10] James E. Tomberlin and Frank McGuinness, "God, Evil, and the Free Will defence," Rel. Stud., 13 (1977), 455-75.

[11] Moral evil is the evil resulting from the free choices of humans or other personal beings (like disembodied spirit, if there are any)--assault, murder, war, and so on. Natural evil is the evil resulting from the processes and events of nature--disease, drought, earthquakes, hurricanes, and so on.

PART II: MORAL EVIL

Nurse: Here's the room, sir.

H: Thanks. You've restored my faith in this place.
I thought that maybe rudeness had become the "in"
style.

Nurse: Oh, I see that you've met our Bessie.

H: That I have. I think you need to do something
about your Bessie.

Nurse: She's really not so bad. Has a terrible bark,
but not much of a bite. Once you get to know her
. . . .

H: I've heard that before. I prefer the kind who are
pleasant on first contact. . . . Anyway, thanks
for showing me to the room. . . . . . . Hey, T,
you trying to hide from me?

T: Well, I did figure that you'd come loaded for bear.
Actually, I think Bessie complained about some of
my friends and had me transferred off her ward. .
. . Can't say that I've shed any tears.

H: C'mon, Bessie's too tough for that. She wouldn't
miss the joys of harassing . . . some of your
friends, as you put it. . . . How's the leg doing?

T: I sure know I've got it! The normal pain stuff
hardly touches it, but I'm not about to go for
anything more powerful. So I guess I just grin
and bear it. . . . How'd your day go?

H: So far, terrible. I have this damned stupid client
who can't stop running off at the mouth once he
gets on the witness stand. Put him on the stand
and he gets a big-star attack. Christ, his case
wasn't worth a flip to begin with, but now it's
completely gone to hell. The reason I'm here now
is that I asked for a recess so I could get the
idiot in hand. . . . The problem is, I really think
he's innocent, but he's doing everything in his
power to blow his case. I spent an hour and a half
with him right after we got out of the courtroom,
but I may as well have been talking to a piece of
sheet-rock. What a jerk!

31

T: Sheet-rock! That reminds me of a group of students during the Vietnam era who made up their minds to drop out of school right after the incursion into Cambodia.

H: That little jog to the west really set off some fireworks, didn't it?

T: You better believe it--literal fireworks, like Kent State. In fact, Kent State was a major reason why these students decided to drop out. They weren't going to finish the semester, even though we were just about into finals. I mean, why worry about college when the whole American system had gone completely to hell? So, off to--guess where?

H: Well . . . where could one go to find instant paradise? Canada . . .? No, the winters are too damn cold . . . and too damn long. I pick California-- the golden state.

T: Right you are, my friend. Their vision was a commune in California. Of course, they didn't have the faintest notion about the commune, how it was to be run or how it was to be financed. Those were utterly trivial matters which could be easily worked out in the spirit of "honesty and acceptance."

H: Yeah, and maybe with a little grass too, right?

T: No, not really. These students weren't much into the drug scene . . . although they were sure drugged by the idea of a commune in California. I'll tell you, I drank more beer--went round and round for hours with them. You know, starting a commune--fine. But at least think through what you're doing. Yet, as you said, talking to sheet-rock .
. . . . . .

H: What ever happened? You keep track of the group?

T: The outcome was . . . really kind of ironic. They burned out pretty quickly on the commune idea--too much freeloading; you know, the old do-your-own-thing business, where my thing is not to do any of the tedious, menial chores, like cleaning up the trash, washing dishes . . . . . .

H: What's ironic about that?

T: Nothing--but I haven't finished. About half the

group ended up on an assembly line in a Ford
plant. Now how's that for a rejection of the cor-
rupt American system?

H: Not a bad way to learn the realities of life--
      speaking of which, by the way . . . .

T: Uh oh, I sense trouble coming my way.

H: Well, I sure have some questions about your theod-
      icy.

T: My friend, I barely got started yesterday. Think
      of how many questions you'll have when I finish.

H: Maybe you won't have to finish.

T: Aha! I see that you have prepared your case
      against me . . . and me without any means of es-
      cape. Maybe I could just faint away . . . or
      better, I could call for Bessie and have her throw
      you out, although . . . yes, maybe the sooner I
      meet my fate the better. Face reality, they say.

H: Right, exactly my words. Seriously, though-------
      now tell me, T--honestly--don't you expect God to
      do more about moral evil? Just take the Holocaust.
      Now if there was ever a time for a loving god to
      intervene, that was it. Yet the absence of even a
      hint of action--the silence, the dead silence--is
      powerful evidence of a god that simply doesn't
      care . . . or, as I think, of no god at all.[1]

T: Permit me to remind you, H, that the Nazi phenom-
      enon called for no small-scale intervention. What
      you seem to be forgetting is that events of the
      scope of the Nazi movement are rooted in a vast
      web of social-environmental conditions and human
      decisions. Changing the events would require in-
      tervention of incredible magnitude on God's part.
      I'm not at all certain that such large-scale inter-
      vention would produce a better human situation in
      the long run. If humans could count on God to bail
      them out whenever things got really intolerable,
      humans might become indolent rather than more res-
      ponsible.

H: Apparently you assume, T, that individuals make
      very little difference in history, that the Nazi
      movement would have hit Germany with its full fury,

Hitler or no Hitler.

T: Sorry, H, but I assume nothing of the sort.

H: Well, let's not argue about the point. Let's just turn to those cases which would obviously not call for massive intervention, cases like Charles Whitman or . . . .

T: Charles Whitman . . . ? Oh yes, he was the fellow who went up the tower at the University of Texas campus and started shooting everybody in sight. Shot over thirty people, as I remember.

H: Right. And then there was Richard Speck, who murdered all those nurses; or more recently that absolutely bizarre situation in Jonestown. In any of these cases merely restraining--I don't say "eliminating" because God could certainly have put the relevant individuals out of commission without completely eliminating them--so as I was saying, merely putting Whitman, Speck, or Jones temporarily out of commission would have meant that today we wouldn't be looking back on some damned grisly events. Now please tell me what would be wrong with that?

T: OK, H, you seem to think that the best way for God to promote responsible freedom is to intervene, to restrain people who are likely to take the lives of many others . . . or to cause considerable suffering. I'm afraid that I'm not ready to go along with your thinking. Take the Jonestown Massacre, for example. The question is: How did Jim Jones get his following? By appealing to critical thought? By stressing rational decision-making? Hardly! He was after true-believers . . . and he got them! His followers were anything but responsible. So what should God have done--intervened? Would that have tended to make mankind more responsible? I hate to say it--call it cruel if you wish--but I fear that many more Jonestowns will have to occur before humans will get after responsible freedom--if they ever will!

H: Get serious, T. What would you have done if you had been in Jonestown with suitable force at hand?

T: I think you're asking the wrong question.

34

H: Yeah, I guess so, if you can't answer it. Look,
    I'm not asking you to do anything more than apply
    the same rules to God that you do to humans.
    Just be consistent. . . . Or are you going to pull
    a TB and resort to mystery?

T: Oh, I have my mysteries, my good friend, as do you;
    but I don't think I have to resort to mystery in
    the present case. . . . You say that I'm letting
    God live by different rules from us. I say, not
    so; and I say that because you and I often act as
    I say that God does--with a hands-off approach.
    For example, to take a relatively trivial case, I
    don't suppose you step in every time your children
    do battle with one another. As a matter of fact,
    I know you don't.

H: Well, I certainly don't try to solve all my chil-
    dren's problems, but if one were about to whack
    another, say, with a metal train, I'd step in.
    You bet I would.

T: But suppose that one of your children is a real in-
    corrigible--always bullying other kids. . . . I'll
    never forget my father saying to me-------you see,
    one of my well-kept secrets (until now) was that
    I went through this stage of thinking I was Mr.
    Tough Guy.

H: Friend Adler would point out that all you've done
    is put on a new suit of clothes, changed the ex-
    terior. On the inside, though . . . .

T: Yes, yes, I know; I'm still Mr. Tough, beating on
    people with my arguments--still trying to compen-
    sate for my sense of inferiority. That theory, my
    good friend, belongs where you and I believe most
    clinical theories belong. Anyway, as I was saying,
    my dad didn't take kindly to my bullying. In fact,
    he became very tired of the complaints from teach-
    ers and other parents. I can still hear him say-
    ing, "I wish you'd get the tar beaten out of you!"

H: Well?

T: Never did. I reformed. Actually, a couple of big
    kids took out after me once for picking on their
    buddy. Fortunately, I had great speed--great in-
    sight, too. I became a confirmed pacifist. . . .
    But getting back to the point . . . .

H: Yes, the point.

T: The point is that my father-------no question
about it; he hoped I'd get beaten on. Yet I don't
begin to think of him as cruel. Indeed, I think
he was correct. I was thoroughly obnoxious, and
a good beating by a peer would have been salutary
medicine.

H: I simply remind you, T, that getting beaten on by
a peer is hardly parallel to getting blown up by
a land mine, or being gassed in an Auschwitz, or
suffering slow death in a slave-labor camp. No,
T, your idea of a hands-off policy just won't
wash; I mean, have you completely forgotten World
War II? Did we just sit on our hands? . . . Or
how about the League of Nations? What was the
coup de grace for the League? Wasn't it the fail-
ure of the League to act in Manchuria . . . and
Ethiopia? Have you ever heard anybody argue that
the world is better today because the League
didn't act? Get serious, T.

T: Not so fast, H. I'm not arguing that a hands-off
policy is always justified, only that it's justified in some instances. I'm sure you've heard the
argument, for example, that the British should cut
out of Northern Ireland. Maybe they should take
the Protestants with them--whichever ones would
go--but they should cut out immediately and completely. Not that a bloodbath of sorts wouldn't
ensue; yet in no other way is a long-range solution likely to be found.

H: A dumb argument, if I ever heard one.

T: I rather think that the argument has a certain
plausibility; but if you want something less controversial, just take the food-population problem
in the Third-World countries.

H: What's less controversial about that? As I see it,
we do a whole hell of a lot for underdeveloped
countries--not as much as we should, by God, but
still a whole hell of a lot.

T: Yes, and my point is that in some cases maybe we
do too much. Look at Bangladesh--ninety four million people jammed into an area the size of Iowa,
which only has about three million people.

36

Bangladesh is surely a very fertile country with a
first-rate climate for agriculture, but no way can
the country support ninety four million people--
not to mention the two million additional mouths
which come on the scene every year. So what should
we or the other developed nations do? Just keep
pumping in aid? Would that be the proper thing to
do?

H: Well, the problem is obviously a very tangled one.

T: The problem requires hard decisions--but tangled?
      How tangled is it, really? Seems obvious to me
      that if we or others just pump in aid, we do noth-
      ing but support further population growth--sort of
      like parents supporting the drug habit of their
      child.

H: Hell, T, that's a wild analogy.

T: Perhaps a bit odious, but not really wild. The
      point is that aid supports a form of undesirable
      behavior. . . . Anyway, the question is, What do
      we do about Bangladesh, particularly if it lacks
      the political will to do anything about its spec-
      tacular population growth? And please remember,
      my good friend, your theory about God is that he
      ought to unilaterally root out certain moral evils.
      Applying your theory to Bangladesh would mean dis-
      pensing with weak-kneed solutions of aid or edu-
      cation which depend on the consent of Bangladesh.
      Who needs consent? We just go in and get the job
      done. . . . Yet as a matter of fact, neither we
      nor anybody else just goes in and gets the job
      done. And we don't for at least two very good
      reasons: first, we realize that some problems
      will never be genuinely solved unless those pri-
      marily affected by the problems take the main res-
      ponsibility for the solutions; and second, we
      think that solving problems autonomously--doing
      things ourselves, independently--is to be highly
      prized.

H: Come on, T, you can do better than that. Your rea-
      sons may sound OK if we're talking about innocuous
      stuff like solving math or dating problems; but
      Jesus, man, we're talking about innocent children
      wandering around with napalm burns, about . . . .
      . . .

T: I think I know perfectly well what we're talking about.

H: Well, you sure do give me reason to wonder. Really, you religious types have a marvelous facility for compartmentalizing your thinking. When humans are involved, you demand love and compassion, but when you come to God--Christ, you get hard as granite. As I said, different rules for God. . . . I'm afraid, T, that I haven't heard anything new from you. You're giving me the same old line that I've heard a thousand times--and it damn sure doesn't get any better with repetition.

T: Relax, H. Maybe you're not listening carefully enough.

H: Listening, hell! Maybe you're the one who's not listening--not listening to the criticism of the old party line.

T: I see we're on a tack which will get us nowhere . . . so maybe I better just continue with my line . . . which you uncharitably referred to as the party line.

H: I take it back. I got carried away.

T: Thank you, my good friend. . . . OK, then--do you remember the two women from Northern Ireland who received the Nobel Peace Prize in . . . '77, I think?

H: It was '76, and their names were Maired Corrigan and Betty Williams.

T: Your memory again proves superior to mine. Cultured for the courtroom, I take it.

H: You could say that.

T: Anyway, what I was about to say is that these two women got motivated--really motivated--by the death of three innocent children. The deaths of the children triggered the women to develop the peace movement which was the basis for the peace prize. Sad to say, the movement never accomplished much. In other words, the harsh reality is that maybe a lot more innocent people will have to die before the factions in Northern Ireland decide to

38

work out a peace.

H: Rot! You'll never get me to swallow your outrageous notions about the suffering of innocent
people.

T: But H, you certainly would agree, wouldn't you,
that sometimes things have to become worse before
they can become better? The death or suffering
of the innocent is unquestionably a tragedy of
immeasurable scope, yet tragedy is often the only
way to get us to be responsible. Besides, I'd
remind you that the death of innocent people can
hardly be avoided, no matter what action we take--
hands-off or otherwise. You tell me, for example,
of some solution in Northern Ireland . . . or in
the Arab-Israeli conflict which would entirely
avoid the suffering and death of innocent people.

H: How about Zimbabwe? . . . OK, I see what you'd
say--while the solution was being worked out and
put into effect, fighting and killing continued.

T: Yes, and continued for some time after the Mugabe
government took power.

H: Granted, but your point is irrelevant. I readily
admit that when we try to straighten things out,
we normally end up with all sorts of complica-
tions. Yet we're talking about God. I should
think that God could pull off a surgically precise
operation.

T: I surely agree, H, that God could pull off a much
neater operation than we. Even so, God would still
have very strong reasons for . . . for keeping his
hands to himself. Remember, your accusation
against me is that I switch rules for God. I've
been trying to show you that I don't do anything
of the sort. My point is that God, just as we,
operates on the principle that some problems will
never be solved unless those directly affected
take primary responsibility for solving the problems; and God, just as we, places a high value on
solving problems autonomously. . . . Another example here would be AA. I would say . . . . . .

H: Your example works in my favor. You surely remember that the first step in the AA program is
to recognize the need for help, to recognize that

you've got a problem you can't handle by yourself.
Do you want to maintain, T--this is, in effect,
what you're maintaining about God--do you want to
maintain that we shouldn't provide help to those
who genuinely want help? That would be insane.

T: Admittedly . . . but let's follow out the analogy
carefully. I'm willing to help a person who ac-
cepts responsibility, who responds to help responsibly. God, then, should also be willing to
provide assistance to a humanity which will respond to his assistance responsibly. The problem
is that the condition has not been met: Humanity
gives few signs of being responsible. God's intervention would probably result simply in a let-
God-do-it attitude.

H: So we're back to square one again. . . . OK, let
me come at this whole thing another way. Take
our criminal justice system. It's based on the
notion of intervention. Now granted the system is
flawed--unbelievably flawed; but I don't know of
anybody who's saying that we ought to go for a do-
nothing approach. I mean, nobody's advocating
anything like that.

T: And therefore I'm not advocating it. . . . I think
I need to go back-------I think my position would
be clearer if I'd just go back and develop my notion of responsible freedom in a bit more detail.
. . . So . . . to begin with, what I'd say is . .
. that responsible freedom consists of a number of
elements. Two fundamental elements are the rational and the moral; or put more simply, the responsible person is one who, among other things, uses
his head and seeks to act in conformity to moral
law.

H: Assuming that there's a single valid set of moral
laws.

T: No, we needn't assume moral objectivity--or value
objectivity, for that matter--for my theodicy to
go. All I need is the admission that the moral and
value goals God is after--goals, let us say, which
I approve--are as acceptable as any other goals
which might be suggested.

H: Hmmmmmm. . . . Accepting moral and value relativism
does give me a bit of a problem in criticizing your

moral and value judgments, doesn't it?

T: I'm glad, my good friend, that you're beginning to
    see the light. . . . But let me continue with what
    I was saying. I was observing that responsible
    freedom has a rational and moral element. Now the
    rational and moral may take several forms. For
    example, I might be moral strictly because I see
    the moral as a supreme value. In other words, I
    might strive to act morally because of a good will,
    because I see moral action as a prize worthy in
    itself. The same goes for the rational. . . . As
    I see things, the motivation of a good will pro-
    vides for the highest . . . and most secure form
    of responsible freedom. What I'd say, then, is
    that God is after the good will as the basis of
    responsible freedom; he'd like to get it, if at
    all possible. In Biblical language, God is after
    a new heart.

H: You mean he wants born-again types, like the ones
    running around on Capitol Hill or in Hollywood or
    . . . .

T: No, not like many of them. You know, as well as
    I, that the media have turned the term 'born-
    again' into a superficial religious slogan. But
    that's another topic. What I want to say now is
    that another form of the moral, a form way at the
    other end of the spectrum from the good will, is
    a form which has to have rewards and punishments
    as props. In other words, a person uses his head
    or adheres to moral law because doing so brings
    some reward, whereas failure to do so means that
    he'll get rapped.

H: I'd hardly call that being responsible. The per-
    son who tells the truth in court because of the
    penalties for perjury is not very responsible--
    at least in my book.

T: Very responsible, right, but responsible, all the
    same. Obviously, we're talking about a low-level
    form of responsibility; yet the person does use
    his head . . . at least to the extent of consider-
    ing some consequences; and he does conform to
    moral norms . . . albeit not from the highest
    motives. But if we had a society of such people,
    we'd have a reasonably livable society.

H: OK, so what's another form of the moral?

T: Well, naturally, I'm not going to list them all.
     I'll just mention one more, one sort of in the
     middle . . . between the good will and rewards
     and punishments. I'm thinking of the businessman
     who says that honesty is the best policy. Now
     here's someone who looks beyond rewards and pun-
     ishments--that is, beyond contrived consequences,
     beyond the artificial, ad hoc, consequences we
     tack on to action. He sees, for example, that
     people don't especially care to be cheated . . .
     and thus they're not about to deal with somebody
     who is likely to take them to the cleaners. Such
     a person, the person functioning on the level of
     natural consequences, has moved up a rung on the
     moral ladder--has moved up from the rung of re-
     wards and punishments. He's looking at a broader
     range of consequences, using his head to a greater
     degree; as a result, he might even begin thinking
     about doing something just because it's right. .
     . . Now as I said, I could go on, distinguishing
     further levels of morality; but I think I've said
     enough to show that the moral is a continuum be-
     tween two extremes. Obviously, then, responsible
     freedom is a similar continuum. The main point,
     of course, is that God is shooting for the highest
     point on the continuum; he's after the maximum in
     responsible freedom. A system of constant inter-
     vention by God, particularly a system heavy on
     punishment, would not, I'd say, be likely to
     achieve the maximum . . . or even the minimum. I'm
     sure you're aware of what reinforcement theorists
     say about punishment.

H: Right. Normally not very effective. Punish one
     kind of undesirable behavior and you may kill it,
     but then another equally undesirable form of be-
     havior is likely to pop up.

T: Yet people seem to attribute a kind of sacredness
     to punishment. You may get somebody who's mis-
     behaving to change his ways, but if you don't
     punish him, somehow you haven't done what you
     should have. Strange! . . . Be that as it may, I
     wanted to mention another element of responsible
     freedom, namely, autonomy. The idea of autonomy
     I want to bring out is that of being self-moti-
     vated, acting from one's own initiative. I'd say,
     for example, that the person who stays off heroin

because of his bare decision to do so exhibits greater autonomy than the person who stays off because of his involvement in a methadone program.

H: OK, I think I get your idea. . . . According to you, then, God is looking for the best combination of morality, rationality, and autonomy.

T: Right, he's aiming for the combination which will be at the highest level of responsible freedom achievable.

H: What do you mean by 'achievable'--the highest level theoretically possible or the highest level . . . well, likely to be achieved?

T: The latter is closer to what I mean, although we'll have to do a bit more digging if you want my precise meaning.

T: No thanks, I'd probably get buried under a mountain of sophistry; and besides, your position has plenty of difficulties right on the surface.

T: I can't recall, though, that you have yet pointed out any really fatal difficulty.

H: Difficulties add up, you know. And one difficulty with what you've been saying is-------I gather from your remarks that God doesn't take the approach we do in our criminal justice system . . . because doing so would not be the way to get to the upper levels of responsible freedom. Yet maybe the upper levels can be reached only by starting on the lower levels--sort of like climbing a mountain.

T: I can see starting on the lower levels. In fact, the Biblical account gives the impression that God did begin at a fairly low level. But he's got to move up . . . and more divine intervention in the way of rewards and punishments or in the way of removing the unmanageable types is not my idea of moving up. Besides, more divine intervention, particularly in the form of punishment, might do nothing but make us more resistant to God's purposes. You'll remember what we said about reinforcement theory and punishment: Punishment just isn't very effective, generally speaking. One reason why it wouldn't be effective in the case

43

of God would be-------I suppose that what we need to remember is the difference in position between God and man.

H: Yeah, I've heard all about that before.

T: But God's position as creator does place him in a different category from man . . . and gives him a different role. You'll surely admit that I, as a professor, have a different role from my students.

H: Granted, but you both have the same goal--or should have. You're after-------you tell me that you want to see your students develop the ability to think critically. Surely, that ought to be their goal too . . . although I guess that for many it isn't.

T: For the majority, my friend--of my students, anyway. But that's another story. What I'm saying now is that I have a different function from my students because of my position. I give them work which <u>they've</u> got to struggle with. I won't do it for them. In fact, if I did, they'd never develop their ability to think. What's more--and this is the main thing I want to emphasize--my position as professor makes me something of an authority figure, with the result that there are certain blocks, certain resistances, to me on the part of the students. Why, just last week--Wednesday, I guess--I was trying to explain this logic problem to a girl--without success. I'd given up when a fellow in the class came along and had her solving the problem in five minutes. A beautiful example of peer teaching.

H: You mean a beautiful confirmation of Freudian theory.

T: No way. The guy is a mousey little fellow, bright as can be but hardly loaded with sex appeal. . . . Anyway, my point is that just as students may have fewer blocks in the case of their peers than in the case of the teacher, so humans may have fewer blocks in the case of interference from other humans--punishment, sanctions, efforts to get reform, things like that--they may have fewer blocks than in the case of God. That humans aren't especially thrilled about divine interference is the constant refrain of the Bible. The more God did to

44

discipline and correct Israel, the more Israel stiffened its neck.

H: Your appeals to the Bible do not impress me, T.

T: Well, maybe not, but I still think the Biblical point is well-taken. In any case, whether we are specially resistant to God's discipline or not, we are plainly not doing very well with the problems of earth. Just take our criminal justice system again. Everybody admits that it has flaws. In fact, the common refrain is that the way to make a person a real criminal is to send him to prison. To be sure, prisons are only one of the weak links in the entire criminal justice chain. The question is, What have we done about the various weak links? Yes, a reform here, a reform there, but nothing like a massive, concentrated effort to make the whole system more effective. Moreover, the criminal justice system is only the flip side of the problem. The front side is . . . getting people off to a proper start. You tell me, though, of any massive programs to strengthen the family. Indeed, we haven't corrected some programs--notoriously, welfare programs--which pursue policies inimical to the family.

H: You're talking about a ton of money, my friend.

T: I'm really talking about priorities, right? So if our priorities are cockeyed--we're not doing what we can or should to get responsible freedom--God surely isn't going to do our work for us. Yes, and I freely admit that many of our programs to get responsible people would have to involve force, yet I think that an overall system could be designed which would achieve fairly high levels of responsible freedom. In any case, we must design and implement the system, not God. Indeed, I'll just reemphasize that if God imposed a system on us, we'd probably just give him the back of the hand.

H: OK, we're not doing what we should. I'm not about to deny that. My problem is that I still can't see what's wrong with a little more divine intervention. Why doesn't God root out and isolate the really disruptive types?

T: If you're thinking of types like Hitler, Stalin,

45

or even Jim Jones, I think, my good friend, I've already answered your question. I thought you despised reruns.

H: Maybe your answer really didn't answer anything.

T: Maybe I need to remind you that I'm not ruling out some intervention by God; I'm not going for a total hands-off policy. Not at all. The Christian view, as you well know, is that God does intervene--he intervenes in redemptive activity, of which Christ is the highest expression. God demonstrates his love-------you see, the appeal of Christ is indirect . . . or maybe I should say, low-key, low-pressure. It's the appeal of love, not a rap on the head. The result for those who seriously respond is a deep commitment to free, autonomous adherence to the law of love.

H: Well, first of all, T, I'd hardly say that God demonstrates his love . . . or anything else. All I see is a vast fog.

T: A slight exaggeration, H. The figure which comes to my mind is that of a dark path. . . . You ever do any night hiking in the high mountains? When the moon is out, no problems. But no moon--the trail just disappears. The only way to keep on the trail is to find the trail signs on the trees. In the Sierras, for example . . . . . .

H: they're cut into the trees, right? A kind of dot, followed by a slash--sort of like an upside-down exclamation mark. I'm an old Eagle Scout, you know.

T: Then you know that finding the signs--you've got to have a flashlight. But finding the signs, even with a flashlight, is anything but easy. . . . My point is that our human pilgrimage is something like going along a Sierra trail on a moonless night: scattered signs, somewhat obscure, yet enough signs to let a person know he's on the trail, enough to keep him going, to keep him searching.

H: Well, I'm sorry, but I haven't seen the signs. As far as I'm concerned, the trail is unmarked.

T: You surely admit mystery in the universe, don't

you? Mystery was one of the most impressive signs of the divine to Einstein.

H: Yes, but the divine for him was anything but an orthodox divine. Besides, I just don't see jumping from mystery to the divine. In fact, unless we're omniscient, we can never rule out a strictly natural explanation of the mysteries, whatever they may be--you know, the old business of trying to prove a universal negative.

T: The fact is--obviously--we're not omniscient, so why not offer tentative explanations? If we have matters which defy naturalistic explanation--we've looked into them carefully but simply can't fit them into our present schemes of natural law and can't see how to alter the schemes in order to bring about a fit--for these matters, why not offer tentative non-natural explanations? Since we're not omniscient, we have no idea what the effects of waiting might be. We could wait an eternity. So I say that we have some things which may, as of now, reasonably be given a non-natural explanation. They're the trail signs.[2]

H: I say, why not wait? Science has continually eliminated mysteries, so why not believe that it will do so in the future? Why make the jump to the divine? The jump is certainly not very parsimonious . . . . What do you call the principle of parsimony--somebody's razor, as I remember.

T: Occam's.

H: Right, Occam's Razor. How'd I forget? So . . . with Occam's Razor I just shave off supernatural explanations. No need to resort to the supernatural if the natural will do.

T: But my point is that when the natural doesn't do, we may resort to the supernatural. Yes . . . we could wait. That's an option I don't believe I can rule out. It seems reasonable to me . . . but so does resorting to the divine, at least under the circumstances I've outlined. Making a tentative, provisional appeal to the supernatural seems perfectly justifiable to me.

H: But what if scientists gave up every time something didn't fit their theories?

47

T: Who said anything about giving up? The very idea
    of a provisional explanation is that you try to
    find out whether it will hold up--you subject it
    to every criticism you can; you look at every
    other explanation available.[3]

H: I still don't agree, T. I was reading something
    the other day about the planet Mercury. Prior to
    Einstein scientists had noted that Mercury's orbit
    did odd things--I mean, what was happening
    couldn't be explained by Newton's gravitational
    principle; and apparently the oddities still
    aren't fully accounted for by Einstein's principle.
    So should we resort to the divine?

T: Since we've already succeeded in reducing the un-
    explained in the case of Mercury, I'd say that we
    have reason to believe in further success. But
    suppose we have . . .let's say, somebody who was
    born blind--and suddenly he gets his sight.

H: I'd be inclined to doubt the reports of his heal-
    ing. The knavery of man is, as David Hume stress-
    ed, always the most reasonable way to account for
    stories of the wonderful and the strange. I'll
    put my money any day on the knavery of my fellow
    humans.

T: Yes, but what if the stories emanated from the
    great skeptic himself, or from Immanuel Kant, or
    from anybody of unquestioned critical acumen and
    integrity? Indeed, what if you didn't have to
    rely on the testimony of others at all, but had
    first-hand knowledge? Suppose-------you know Max
    out at school?

H: Do I know Max? Who doesn't? He's into everything
    in the community-------excuse the pun; totally un-
    intentional, I assure you. . . . I hear the guy's
    got two--not one, but two--torrid affairs going,
    along with other occasional liaisons.

T: You've heard right on that, my friend. I'm afraid
    that Max is obsessed with proving that his handi-
    cap is no handicap at all. He runs long distance
    races, paints, plays jazz piano--you name it. . .
    . Anyway, what I want to say is, suppose that you
    had been his physician from birth. You'd examined
    him thoroughly many times. You had a pile of re-
    cords from tests of all sorts, showing

48

unambiguously that his optical system was totally deficient. He just wasn't born with the necessary equipment. But now suppose that a faith healer comes to town . . . or that he gets prayed for by some religious group--and gets healed. Just like that! Sees perfectly. What would you say in a case like that?

H: I don't think that anything like that has occurred, does occur, or will occur.

T: Right now we're not talking about what is actually the case. We're talking about the kind of event which would provide reasonable grounds for a tentative projection of the divine.

H: Well, I still don't see the big difference between your example and my example of Mercury.

T: I've already mentioned a difference, although maybe it's not big enough for you. In any case, don't lose my point about Max. What I'm saying in his case is that you'd have the testimony of your own senses, plus records of examinations using the most modern techniques of medicine, records you could check and recheck. I think you'd have every reason to believe that a man born blind had gained his sight. But you wouldn't have a naturalistic explanation. Yes, and let's suppose that in the twenty-second century we still wouldn't have a naturalistic explanation. Actually, we don't need to wait until the twenty-second century because we've already had plenty of time to come up with an explanation. Reports of Max-type events have been around for who knows how long? Take, for example, the story in the Gospel of John.

H: Hell, T, nobody tries to come up with scientific explanations for far-out stories--for events based on triple hearsay evidence.

T: Oh, lots of people have attempted to explain many of the miracles of the Bible--but not the healing of somebody born blind. That kind of happening, along with a number of other kinds, just seems resistant to a naturalistic interpretation. And besides-------do you want a full-fledged discussion of miracles? If so, you better forget my theodicy.

49

H: On with your theodicy, T. I think I can take a rain check on miracles.

T: Well, I really didn't mean to get off into miracles. For one thing I wouldn't limit mystery to what is normally viewed as miracle. Of course, mystery isn't the only way to get to the divine--at least according to many theists. In any case, I'm just saying that some aspects of the universe provide for a tentative resort to the divine. Actually, I'm most impressed with religious experience. That, to me, is the most significant and convincing sign of the divine.

H: Jesus, T, nothing like hopping from one controversial issue to another; but you better not expect me to hop with you . . . because I want to get back to the signs--the trail signs, as you call them. Please be so kind as to inform me as to why God has to resort to obscurity. I mean, a series of Max-type events would probably make even me a little more inclined to be religious. So what's up with God? What's his game--cosmic hide and seek?

T: To be as succinct as I can, ambiguity is, I'd say, the very stuff of an exciting, adventuresome religion. I'm with Whitehead when he says that religion is an adventure of the spirit.[4] Now adventure surely involves uncertainty, excitment, risk, daring: The route isn't clearly charted; hostiles may be in the area; a hidden reef may be struck. Yes, indeed--God could reduce the uncertainty, the risk. He could, if you will, put on an Elijah-like demonstration every five years. I simply maintain, though, that a religion in which uncertainty--ambiguity--is eliminated is a religion of far less adventure than what we now have. Moreover, I maintain that a religion of adventure is far better than a religion robbed of the unexpected, the unknown, the surprising. I'm not going to claim that my value judgment is indisputable, but
 . . . .

H: I know, I know, the same old refrain: Your value judgment is plausible--as plausible as its denial. . . . But if a religion of uncertainty and risk is so great, how about Moses . . . or St. Paul? I mean, a burning bush or a flash out of the sky is hardly the way to maintain ambiguity.

T: Yes, but don't forget the trail signs! Moses and
      Paul were exceptional cases--surely, that's the
      Biblical view. Yet we need exceptional cases. We
      definitely need signs of the divine which are
      clear enough to get us started . . . and to keep
      us going on the religious adventure--a burning
      bush here, a flash out of the sky there. . . .
      Now please don't interpret me with wooden literal-
      ness.

H.   My good friend, you wound me deeply. I am not a
      freshman student, you know.

T: Oh, my most sincere apologies. How could I have
      had such a lapse? Must have been a conditioned
      response . . . or maybe I had a clandestine shot
      of something.

H: Well, please make a heroic effort to get yourself
      back under rational control. . . . Anyway, getting
      back to the issue, I suppose the only thing for
      me to do is . . . return to the question I raised
      at the very start of our conversation. What about
      Whitman-type cases? How would divine intervention
      in such cases be detrimental in the least?

T: I guess the best way to answer your question is to
      return to what I said about God's role. God's
      role is to get us to be responsible. Our role is
      to be responsible--to tackle and solve the pro-
      blems facing us, to cut the procrastination, the
      excuses, the scapegoating, the whining. We're to
      roll up our sleeves and get with it. Now in order
      to get us to be responsible, God is obviously not
      going to solve our problems for us. In fact, he
      may go to the limits of his restraint just to get
      us to do what we should. . . . I recall an inci-
      dent at the university pool. My children had
      invited a neighbor girl to the pool with them.
      She definitely wasn't about to win any medals with
      her swimming; all the same, she was down at the
      deep end, jumping off the small board as if there
      were no tomorrow. After going off the board one
      last time, she began to struggle. I was fully
      aware of her problems; kept my eyes glued on her,
      when--she was now only about five feet from the
      edge of the pool--in jumps a student and drags
      her out of the pool. He stands looking at me as
      if I'm some sort of irresponsible fool. . . . You
      see, I was letting the girl go the limit. I

thought the lesson would be valuable--not soon
forgotten. To this day I don't see the student's
behavior as better than mine, although . . . . .
.

H: I'd probably have done what you did, but we're not
talking about anything like the situation you des-
cribe. If the girl had started to go under, you
certainly would have jumped in. I'm saying that
we're going under--we've been on the way down for
some time; yet God continues in his stance of
benign neglect--only I don't think the neglect is
so benign.

T: On that point, my good friend, I'm not especially
sanguine about our coming to a meeting of the
minds. Yet really, we don't have to. All that I
want you to admit is that my position, that God's
neglect is benign (indeed, benevolent), that sometimes benevolence requires letting things go pretty far-------all I want is the admission that my
position is as reasonable as yours.

H: Well, let me come back to Whitman. Now just what
could we have done to stop him? Looking at his
background, you'd think he was the all-American
boy. There just wasn't any way we could have iso-
lated him beforehand; nor was anybody able to stop
him before he had shot, as we said, over thirty
people. Now that's a bunch of people!

T: It sure is. But you have to remember a couple of
things. First of all, you'll recall that I've
introduced the notion of ambiguity--trail signs
and all that.

H: So God's signs are ambiguous. How does that-----
--OK, I see what you're up to. Taking care of the
Whitman-type cases would reduce ambiguity.

T: Exactly.

H: My obvious response is: So what? Reducing ambiguity is surely preferable to permitting extensive death and suffering.

T: A debatable point.

H: Good God, T, you can't be serious. There's not a
parent alive who would let his child risk injury

or death just so that the child would search for answers.

T: So you don't think that the risks of ignorance are worth the benefits of the search for truth; that, for example, the condition of ignorance, which gives rise to science, is worth the benefits of the scientific enterprise? If you had created man, you would have given him the straight story on everything right from the beginning! . . . Yes, I think your point is debatable. I say that the search for truth is a high value, worth considerable suffering. And that goes for religious, as well as scientific, truth. As for Whitman-type cases, God's refusal to intervene may be seen as a stimulus to further investigation, a stimulus to greater responsibility. . . . Actually, I can even grant that God should intervene in such cases . . . provided the conditions are right, provided humans are doing everything in their power to search for knowledge and to establish a responsible society.

H: Well, as a matter of fact, nobody could have done anything in the case of Whitman. As I remember, they discovered a tumor in his brain.

T: But who says that the tumor was the cause of his action? My neighbor is undergoing radiation therapy now for a brain tumor, and she doesn't even get irritable!

H: That's beside the point. What I'm saying is that behavior which has a cause we couldn't possibly know about . . . . . .

T: Why couldn't we come to know? Any reason in principle why we couldn't develop adequate methods, screening methods, to determine whether or not some physical condition--a condition which causes undesirable behavior--whether or not that condition is present? I see no reason why we couldn't . . . . Anyway, my main point-------as I was saying, I could grant that if humans were responsible, God would be obligated to intervene in a Whitman-type case. Of course, I'm not going to grant this because of what I said about ambiguity. Yet if I did grant it, all I'd have to do is observe that, as a matter of fact, humans are generally so irresponsible, so incapable of moving unless an

53

overwhelming crisis is at hand-------do I have to spell it out? And there's still another point. If God's intervention is not to be deleterious, humans must be able to see very clearly that they could not have foreseen or prevented what took place. Seeing such a thing, though, is in most cases extremely difficult, if not impossible, for the sophisticated and intellectually honest, not to mention the untrained and the lazy. If God were to intervene in situations which would be mis-interpreted-------well, you know the result, as well as I.

H: Yes, H, your point--much as I hate to admit it--your point is well-taken. But I guess you're per-mitted a good point every now and then.

T: Are you getting exhausted, my friend? A compli-ment! I'm not sure I can handle that.

H: Just say, thank you.

T: Thank you. . . . But I also want to say something else. There's another reason why God might not intervene . . . even if we should be generally re-sponsible. God might not intervene just . . . just to remind us of our finitude.

H: Oh Christ, T! You go from the sublime to the ridi-culous. Now you're talking like TB.

T: Well, not everything that TB says is wild, you know. In any case, I think that the idea of fini-tude is crucial to being really human. Indeed, a basic thesis of the Genesis account of man's fall is that man wanted to be what he wasn't--he wanted to be like God. My view is that a healthy sense of our finitude is necessary for living life res-ponsibly. It would surely cut down on our pater-nalistic efforts, most of which . . . .

Nurse: Sir, you'll have to go now. It's a half hour past visiting hours. I have to run some tests on . . . .

H: Jesus! . . . Oh, excuse me--I mean, I'm sorry. I completely lost track of the time.

Nurse: No real problem. You weren't interfering with anything. But now, as I was saying, I have to run some tests on your friend.

H: Well, isn't this something to behold--a real study
    in contrasts. What we needed, T, was a video sys-
    tem to tape yesterday and today--how not to do it,
    and how to do it. You could have packaged the
    tape and sold it to the school of health sciences
    there at the university.

T: Not a bad idea. I've been thinking of going to
    half-time or cutting out altogether; so I could
    use the money.

H: You . . . cutting out of teaching? You better tell
    me more about that. . . . OK, nurse, I'm leaving.
    Let's see, what's your name? . . . Jan? OK, Jan,
    I'm on my way. Just be careful with T here on
    those tests. He's a very sensitive soul.

T: Right, but he has a very tough body. . . . Take it
    easy, H.

H: Yeah, see you soon.

T: By the way, everything still set for speaking to
    my class a week from Thursday?

H: You going to be back at school by then?

T: May have to fudge on a test or two, but Jan here
    looks like the cooperative type.

H: Well, I'll be there. I've got it down on my calen-
    dar. So long.

T: Auf wiedersehen.

NOTES

[1]See, for example, Elie Wiesel's Night (New York: Discus
Edition, Avon Books, 1969), pp. 44, 76.

[2]Richard L. Fern holds that the abnormality of an event, the
fact that it cannot be explained in a naturalistic framework, is
only a necessary condition for a miracle and cannot provide
grounds for believing in a supernatural explanation. "It is only

55

when we turn to the factor of purposefulness that we find dis-
criminating reasons in support of the belief that a miracle has
occurred." (Richard L. Fern, "Hume's Critique of Miracles: An
Irrelevant Triumph," Rel. Stud., 18, 1982, 351.) The crucial
question is, How does one demonstrate that an event in the physical world manifests purpose? Many biological events which were
viewed as purposive prior to Darwin are no longer so viewed. In
other words, if we wish to show purpose (supernatural purpose),
we must do exactly what we must do in the case of abnormal events:
We must rule out strictly naturalistic explanations. The route
going from the apparently purposeful (the event could be purposeful or could be given a purposeful interpretation) is plagued by
the same epistemic problems as the route going from abnormalities
to the supernatural. I do not wish to deny that a miracle must
exhibit supernatural purpose. My only point is that showing
supernatural purpose by way of some event in the natural world is
no less difficult and indecisive than showing supernatural power
by way of some abnormal event.

[3]See Karl R. Popper, Objective Knowledge (Oxford: At the
Clarendon Press, 1972), chpt. 1.

[4]Alfred N. Whitehead, "Religion and Science," in Interpretation of Science (New York: Bobbs Merrill, 1961), p. 183.

PART III: NATURAL EVIL

H: That's one fine class you have, T. They asked some damn good questions--thoughtful questions.

T: Well, I'd given them a pile of reading to do while I was in the hospital, so they were primed. . . . But they <u>are</u> a first-rate class. Not really super bright . . . but hard workers. Probably the best class I've had in the last three or four years.

H: Say, tell me, if I may change the subject------- you mentioned in the hospital that you might cut out of teaching for a while. What's up?

T: No "might" about it any more. I've made up my mind--and my wife agrees--I'm taking a two-year leave. A couple of reasons. I've been fed up for some time with having to teach courses out of my field. You know, I've told you about the composition courses I've had to teach . . . and how they're really little more than remedial courses. I mean, just look at this from my standpoint. You went into law to practice law, right? How'd you like to be working as a court recorder . . . or legal secretary . . . or . . . . . .

H: I get your point.

T: Don't get me wrong. I go for teaching . . . but in <u>my</u> field, in philosophy. . . . Actually, though, the last straw was-------I'm being pressured to go into administration . . . which I dearly despise.

H: But how would that be so bad? You'd probably end up with a cushy job . . . at a higher salary.

T: You're right. The salary would be higher, but I'd only be teaching one course a semester, with no assurance that it would be philosophy. . . . Nope, I'm going to try something else.

H: Am I permitted to be nosy?

T: Why not? You know that frogurt place on the north end of town?

H: The Purple Cow?

57

T: Right. As a matter of fact, the place was owned by your friend--what's his name?

H: Gene Adams. . . . Did you buy the place?

T: We're going to sign the papers next week. . . . By the way, whatever happened to Gene? I remember seeing him at a couple of political affairs . . . and then bang! I see his picture on the obituary page . . . with no explanation except that he had a brief illness.

H: Eaten up by cancer. They opened him up and found his stomach and liver just gone. He died within a month. I'd played tennis with him just two weeks before he had surgery. Seemed all right to me . . . although we did lose our doubles match.

T: That, my friend, was probably your doing. . . . Didn't Gene have a number of children--five or six?

H: Six. All boys. He was pretty well set, though, financially. I must say that his death just devastated the family. They haven't begun to get over it yet.

T: One of those real shockers in life.

H: One of those faith-killers, I'd say--that is, if people of faith would only let themselves think for a moment.

T: I see you're spoiling for an argument. That session with my class must've primed you.

H: Listen, my fine-feathered friend, I'm continually primed on this issue. What I'd like to know, really like to know, is . . . .

T: Oh, hello, M [Mystic]. You looking for a place to sit?

M: Well, I'd definitely just as soon not stand and drink my coffee.

T: Be our guest. . . . This is my friend, H. . . . H, meet M, one of my fine colleagues.

H: Pleased to meet you.

M: Likewise. . . . Wasn't your picture in the paper recently? You were the defense lawyer in that bizarre Wimberly case, correct?

H: Correct. You see, the more bizarre the case the better the publicity.

M: Well, that was one very bizarre case, I'll say that!. . . . How's the leg, T?

T: Not bad. A slight infection--probably picked it up in the hospital. But everything is pretty well under control. Should be back to normal in a decade or so.

M: Right. Need to pump all you can out of the insurance agency. Or better, how about a little suit?

T: I think I'd have a case. I discovered that the bolts holding the blade on the edger should have had reverse threads . . . but they didn't. A lock-washer couldn't even begin to hold the nuts.

H: I told you that you're boy in Beulah was bad news.

M: I take it that H is here to talk to you about a suit.

T: No, H is here because he talked to my class about capital punishment. . . . Did an outstanding job. A very stimulating class session.

M: Wish I could say the same for my last class.

T: Well, stick around. We may have something going that you'll enjoy. H and I have been getting after the problem of evil now for about two weeks. H was just in the process of starting a cross-examination of me.

M: Sounds interesting. Go right ahead with your cross-examination, H. I'll just be a spectator.

H: No, join in. The more the merrier. . . . Actually, what I was about to do was ask a question about natural evil.

M: You mean earthquakes, hurricanes, disease--things like that?

59

H: Right. All those natural processes and events which bring suffering to humans. . . . Now people usually rationalize natural evil . . . .

T: 'Explain' is the word, my friend. Don't beg the question.

M: I think T is right.

H: Rationalize! They rationalize natural evil by saying that it builds virtue or moral character. Yet any virtue arising from the fires of natural evil could equally well arise from the fires of moral evil. So why two fires when one would do?

T: Good question, H. First of all, I agree with your basic premise . . . your implicit premise that God may not permit any more suffering than is necessary to bring about responsible freedom. His experiment . . . .

M: Experiment? What's this--God's conducting an experiment?

T: Yes, M--my view is that the present world order is something of an experiment, an attempt by God to achieve responsible freedom.

M: I declare! When you believe in a deity fashioned in man's image, there's no telling where you'll end up.

H: T likes adventure, so he doesn't mind ending up in strange places.

T: M, I realize that on your view God is an impersonal reality, not at all similar to man. Naturally, if God is impersonal, he--or it--is neither good nor evil, but strictly amoral. With an amoral deity you don't have to bother about explaining evil. That's surely a plus; but the minus is that an impersonal deity------how much time do you have?

H: M, you're going to let T off the hook--my hook. He'll start arguing with you rather than answer my question. He's tricky enough when he stays on the question.

M: Oh, my apologies, H. We surely wouldn't want T

to get off easy. I give the floor back to you.

H: The floor is really T's. I've already asked my
    question.

T: All right, H, you say, in effect, that natural
    evil is redundant. I say, not so. To begin with,
    natural evil provides further occasions on which
    freedom can respond, further occasions for putting
    freedom to the test . . . and thus it provides
    for, among other things, a quicker revelation of
    the course of freedom. In addition, natural evil
    provides further stimuli--stimuli to be respon-
    sible. Yes, and the testing and stimulus func-
    tions of natural evil are qualitatively different
    from those of moral evil. In other words, people
    may very well respond differently--more positive-
    ly, perhaps--to natural evil than to moral evil.

H: T, your whole idea of natural evil as a stimulus
    is strained at best--mere wishful thinking. Hell,
    just take the floods which hit the Midwest last
    spring. They really stimulated freedom to be
    responsible, didn't they? Farmlands inundated,
    the economy in a shambles, people homeless, fami-
    lies decimated. Great stimuli, these natural
    disasters!

M: You are engaging in rhetoric, H. Most of what
    you say is entirely beside the point.

H: Beside the point! Christ Almighty--I mean, ex-
    cuse me . . . but . . . .

M: You needn't worry that my ears are unaccustomed
    to profanity . . . or to shoddy reasoning, for
    that matter. Apparently you don't see--or are
    conveniently forgetting--the complicity of humans
    in so-called natural disasters. Most natural
    evils are evil just because of sheer human stupi-
    dity.

T: Good point, M.

H: Well, of course, human stupidity is involved,
    but . . . .

M: No but's. Human stupidity is involved--egregious
    human stupidity. People place themselves in risk
    situations and then curse the universe when the

61

risk comes.

H: Nonsense. Most people live where and how they do out of economic necessity.

M: Double nonsense. People live where they do for a whole variety of reasons. They may live in an area simply because they were brought up there . . . or perhaps for religious reasons. What's more, many of them won't move, no matter what the danger, be it earthquake, fire, or flood. Just take the earthquakes which recently hit southern ▸ Italy. The government tried to move people from especially dangerous areas, but many of them wouldn't budge. They weren't going to leave the city of their fathers, not even for a brief time.

H: All right, so some of the people in southern Italy wouldn't move. Let's talk about here. What I'd like to know is . . . how people on welfare or marginal incomes are supposed to relocate . . . or spend money to improve the safety of their homes--which most of them don't own, anyway.

M: The safety of the poor is only one aspect of a much larger problem--the treatment of the weak and deprived in society.

T: You're so right, M. You see, H, the problem is really a problem of moral evil. However, the topic, as I recall, is supposed to be natural evil. . . . The point M and I are making about nature is that-------admittedly, it has negative aspects, yet overall it's essentially neutral . . . although I'm inclined to say that on balance it's good.

H: Surprise!

T: Yes, surprise! . . . Look, I say that nature is good because it's ordered--things don't just happen in any old fashion. Indeed, it's ordered in such a way that we can adjust to it and work with it for our benefit. Just think for a moment about this matter of adjusting to nature. We know, for example, that we live in a hurricane area. Now we can either build and plan with this reality in mind, or we can say, "To hell with it all." In fact, when we hear of an approaching hurricane, we can gather all our friends for a party. Some people actually did that during hurricane Camille. Not a trace of them was found.

H: OK, OK, I don't dismiss the stupidity of humans. I just think we have enough trouble with moral evil. You're going to have to do a lot more to convince me that we need the further hassle of natural evil.

T: Don't forget that natural evil is closely linked with moral evil. Most of the harm we do people is done because all of us have bodies which are integral parts of a lawful nature. Change this nature so that our bodies can't be harmed and you'd automatically cut out most moral evil. Of course, you could cut natural evil in our present system of nature by way of more divine intervention, but in that case ambiguity would be reduced. Hopefully, though, you remember my ambiguity argument.

H: Yes, I remember.

M: Well, I certainly don't.

H: T has this fine theory that God plays his cards close to his vest--keeps people guessing. Or perhaps I should say, keeps blowing smoke in their face.

T: My view, M--if we may achieve some degree of accuracy--my view is that the pursuit of God, searching for God, is far superior to having everything mapped out for us in detail. If God were easily and readily known, if uncertainty and mystery were eliminated, so would be much of the adventure and excitement of religion.

M: Yes, I definitely see religion as a search--but . . . uncertainty? What about the experience of God? Nothing uncertain about that!

T: I grant that the experience may leave a person <u>feeling</u> very certain, yet the fact that we may question whether the experience was really of God . . . .

M: That's a question which only those who have never had the experience can raise.

63

T: The fact that mystics ignore the question--or con-
     sider it naive--doesn't mean the question can't
     legitimately be raised. I fully understand that
     a person's sense of inner certainty may simply sti-
     fle all questions. Yet the questions still must
     be asked: Is the inner certainty justified? Was
     the encounter really with God? I say that the
     sense of God's presence is no more self-authenti-
     cating than the sense of anything else--of impend-
     ing doom, of some other person's presence in the
     room, you name it. I mean, how do you explain the
     conflicts? Not everybody seems to encounter the
     same divinity, you know.

M: T, I'm afraid you have very little understanding
     of mystic experience.

H: Excuse me for interrupting, but . . . M, you're
     permitting T to take a detour. He's undoubtedly
     happy to do so . . . just to avoid my questions.
     But if you'll recall, this conversation is about
     natural evil, not religious or mystic experience.

M: Oh, my apologies again--my sincere apologies.

T: I should have warned you, M; H is tough. No fool-
     ing around with him--deviate from the issue and
     he whacks you back in line. . . . I think you and
     I will have to discuss mystic experience another
     time--unless we can catch H napping.

H: No chance, my friend, no chance at all.

T: Getting back to what I was saying, then, let's
     suppose . . . let's just suppose that we had a
     different nature--a more benign . . . a more
     forgiving nature. Such a nature would provide us
     with little incentive to be responsible. Or may-
     be I should say, the necessity of being responsible
     would be largely eliminated. I mean, consider a
     nature in which I could do little to harm myself
     or others--if I shot someone, the wound would
     immediately heal; if I built a large condominium
     right next to a river, the river would never flood;
     and so on.

H: Doesn't sound bad to me.

M: Don't be silly, H. Such a nature would give you
     little reason to be concerned about yourself or

others. It would be the occasion for nothing but moral flabbiness.

T: You took the words right out of my mouth, M. The kind of nature I described would require little of moral consequence of anybody. As things now stand, the pressure is on--I am put to constant moral test.

M: Yes, and I might add, you will receive the exact moral consequence due each action. I suppose that you'd accept the notion of karma, wouldn't you?[1] I admit that it's broader than your notion of nature, but . . . . . .

T: Suffice it to say, M, I'm very sympathetic to the notion of karma. But to hew to the issue--H isn't even showing a tendency to doze--so, to hew to the issue, I'd say that nature as we now have it tests us, puts the pressure on us, stimulates us; and it does so in ways that people don't. In other words, I'm back to my point that natural evil is qualitatively distinct from moral evil. . . . Maybe an example would help here. I read about a case some time ago--had to do with a typhoon, with what we on the Gulf call a hurricane. I guess the time was '75 or '76. The typhoon came roaring across the island of Guam, devastating just about everything that wasn't made of solid concrete. You'd have thought that the islanders would've been in shock and despair, traumatized over the loss of just about everything they pos- sessed. What happened, though, is that they im- mediately banded together, got after the task of cleaning up, repairing, and rebuilding--and I do mean 'got after'. No eight to five, ho-hum af- fair. They pulled out all the stops. Often worked around the clock.

H: So what's all this have to do with your point? You've shown at best that the typhoon stimulated some socially useful activity. You surely haven' shown that the typhoon did what moral evil couldn't or wasn't likely to do.

T: I haven't shown that because I haven't finished. The really astonishing thing was the total turn- around in the attitude of the islanders. Prior to the typhoon they were divided into factions, bickering over everything, doing absolutely

65

nothing to solve very serious problems in their educational system and their economy. The typhoon, though, turned everything around. In other words, prior to the typhoon moral evil--I'd count a deteriorated educational system, for example, as a moral evil. An educational system goes to the devil largely because of neglect, sheer self-interest, empire-building, myopic decision-making, amateurish management, and a whole array of other strictly human factors.

H: T, your argument won't wash. The same results could have been obtained by, let's say, a war or the threat of war.

T: Not if the war had left the island with an occupying force. At any rate, don't forget, a war just wasn't around, whereas the typhoon did come roaring in. You see, I can at least say that moral evil alone leaves gaps in the stimulus pattern. Natural evil fills the gaps. . . . However, there's something else to mention. Natural evil is, I should say . . . more controllable--I mean, more controllable than humans, particularly if humans have the freedom of indeterminism. Nature is regular, predictable, and . . . impersonal. It really is qualitatively different from the human. . . . That's hardly even arguable. So if nature is qualitatively different, what's fanciful about saying that our response to nature is likely to be different--that our response to the impersonal is not going to be the same as our response to the personal? For example, although I may very well become hostile and angry toward people, I'm far less likely to have these feelings toward nature. As a result, my response in the case of natural evil might be far more constructive than in the case of moral evil.

H: OK, T, let's suppose that what you say is true. Just so we don't go round and round, I'll grant-- I mean, I'm being extremely generous--but I'll grant that natural evil is not redundant. OK? But I'll tell you something else that natural evil is not: It's not distributed properly. In my book a good god would deploy the stimuli of natural evil in an optimum fashion; he'd concentrate on those who would be likely to respond positively. But do you find even the slightest trace of an optimum distribution? Do hurricanes, earthquakes, and epidemics hit only those who are likely to respond positively?

M: H, the idea of God's distributing anything is crass, primitive.

H: I might agree with you on that, but remember: We're talking about T's god, not yours.

T: Obviously, M, the whole idea of a personal god seems crass to you; but I think we decided not to discuss that issue. . . . Admittedly, I'm defending a form of personal theism--crass, sophisticated, whatever it is, I'm defending it, trying to show that the goodness of God is tenable.

M: Yes, I think I have the picture. In fact, I'm very interested in seeing what you can do. Naturally, I don't accept your brand of theism. All the same, you were saying . . . ?

T: Actually, H was the one saying something. He was saying that God should distribute natural evils to those who would be likely to respond positively. I think, H, you really need to narrow down your thesis. M and I have argued that many natural phenomena become evil strictly because of human irresponsibility. We might have to modify our argument for an earlier time . . . but I'm thinking of the present. Now in the present the distribution problem is raised, I'd say, only by those natural phenomena which we moderns, even with our best efforts, cannot yet avoid--for example, certain diseases and birth defects. Maybe we could concentrate just on disease. . . . According to you, H, God should follow a more selective system, a rifle rather than a shotgun approach. . . . I suppose that the immediate reply to you would be, disease --actually, natural evil of all forms, but certainly disease--disease could be justified strictly on the ground that it puts pressure on humans to seek knowledge.

H: As if we couldn't investigate nature without being continaully drubbed and pummelled.

T: It's not what we could or might do, but what we have done, are doing, and are likely to do. Besides, I don't think we're drubbed or pummelled. I'd say that disease is more like a goad . . . maybe like

67

a jab in the ribs. Whatever the figure, though, the fact is that disease puts the pressure on us to understand our world--something which is absolutely essential for responsible action. I hardly need add that our struggle for knowledge has been anything but heroic. The Parable of the Cave is an apt description of humankind.[2] We're not about to leave our cherished shadows to go up into the light. . . . No, H, I think we need a goad--a constant, universal irritant--to keep us moving.

H: But why universal? That's just my question. Why not something more selective?

T: Aside from the ambiguity problem . . . .

H: You're getting an awful lot of mileage out of that.

T: You're going to be surprised how much mileage! At any rate, here's what I'd say about an impartial, non-selective distribution system. First of all, you need to remember that the distribution of disease is relevant to others besides the individual directly affected. The question is not merely, How will he respond to adversity? but also, How will others respond? What will their reaction be? You see, I may be affected far more by illness to my child, a loved one, a friend, or a personality of note-------I may be far more affected by what happens to them than by what happens to me. The fact that disease strikes impartially places a kind of general pressure on me. Since anybody can be affected, including me, I'm constantly given an incentive to do something about disease.

H: You'd be given the same incentive in a selective distribution system. People would still be getting disease, and some of the people might be close to you.

T: Right . . . people would still be getting disease, unless they were weak, unlikely to respond with courage, nobility of spirit, or personal growth. Indeed, the way to avoid disease would be to remain in a state unlikely to provide for growth in responsibility. As it is, disease strikes without consideration of one's likely response. The only way to avoid disease is to do something about it-- all the way from watching your own health carefully

68

to donating to medical research. In other words, the only way to avoid disease or cope with it is to act responsibly. A selective system would put far less pressure on us to be responsible. As a result, H, I'd have to maintain that our present arrangement is superior to your proposed arrangement.

M: I might just add that disease--or perhaps I should say, suffering in general--suffering is a major incentive to seek values of a more lasting nature, an incentive to turn from the ephemeral, the illusory, to the real.

H: Rot! Why couldn't people seek the so-called true values--whatever the exact list may be--why couldn't people seek these values apart from suffering? Many do, as a matter of fact. . . . And you better not forget those who are driven by suffering to indulge themselves fully--you know, eat, drink, and carouse, for tomorrow you too may be suffering.

M: Who said that everybody responds appropriately to suffering?

T: Obviously, everybody doesn't . . . but let me finish what I wanted to say. . . . Supposing that everything I've said in defense of the present system of distribution is worthless, I could just maintain that God can't do what you want him to, H--distribute natural evil only to those who are likely to respond positively. He can't do this because he simply can't determine who would be likely to respond positively.

H: I swear, T, you're just like an eel. You get caught on one point, and you slither off to another.

M: I see, T, that your god has limited knowledge. I guess I should have gathered as much from the fact that this world is an experiment.

T: Right. We're assuming that humans are indeterminately free and that God can't know an indeterminate future. He can make projections . . . but the point I was just about to make was that he can't very well make projections without data. If a person hasn't suffered yet, God has no previous instances to go on. . . . As I recall, H, in one of

our previous conversations you voiced an argument
along this line. Right?

H: Well . . . uh . . . .

T: I could also say that God has greater difficulty
     projecting individual than group behavior, just
     as the behavior of an individual sub-atomic par-
     ticle . . . . . .

H: Now you're grasping for straws.

M: Oh, I don't think T's argument is so bad. Per-
     haps you've just run out of objections, H. But
     if I may intrude for a moment . . . if I may ask
     just one question-------is that permissible, H?

H: Well, maybe I ought to appoint a committee-------
     yeah, sure, go ahead.

T: Before you ask your question, M, let me just clar-
     ify what I think has happened. I don't think I've
     demonstrated conclusively that a non-selective
     distribution system is better than a selective sys-
     tem for achieving responsible freedom; or, more
     generally, I don't think I've conclusively justi-
     fied our present system. But then, I don't have
     to. You'll remember, H, that all I have to do is
     . . . .

H: Come on, T, I'm not senile, you know.

T: Well, maybe my impressions are misleading me, but
     I have the feeling that you expect my arguments
     to be better than yours. . . . You see, M, in a
     theodicy a person simply has to show that his
     views are as plausible as their denials. He
     doesn't have to show their superiority. . . . But
     now, you had a question.

M: Yes, here's my question. You say, T, that the
     present system of natural evil is non-selective.
     I take it, though, that you're orthodox enough to
     admit an occasional intrusion by God. You'd admit
     to miracles, wouldn't you?

H: Yes, indeed. God's got to tinker with his world.
     You see, God couldn't get it right to begin with.[3]

T: My good friend, if you're intending to voice a

70

serious objection, you've failed miserably. There's no reason whatsoever why God's plan to do things right, to get as good a universe as possible, could not include what you call tinkering. Naturally, the term 'tinkering' is a bit question-begging, so I'd dispense with it. The only question is whether God's creation of the present order is justified. The present order, by reason of the fact that it's designed to achieve responsible freedom, includes everything that would be most useful in reaching that goal. If you want to make a serious objection, you will have to show that divine intervention is not useful, that a total hands-off policy would be more likely to succeed than the limited hands-off policy that we now have. Unfortunately, your whole argument is that God should intervene more, not less. Or have you forgotten?

H: No, T, I haven't forgotten. Besides, my whole argument, as you put it, is really that God should have begun with a better world, a heavenly world.

T: But possibly a heavenly world is better--I'm thinking here of natural evil--perhaps a heavenly world is free of natural evil only because of constant divine intervention. In other words, maybe our present natural order is as benign as an order can be apart from extensive miracle.

H: Get serious, T.

T: I'm completely serious. You see, you seem to think that God's omnipotence provides him with a blank check, that God can create a world with any and every property which strikes our fancy . . . . Afraid not! For example, God can't create a spatial object which can be in two places at the same time. Neither can God create a world in which all possibles are realized. . . . Let's suppose that a world in which nature functions unpredictably is as possible as our present world, a world in which nature is regular and ordered. Obviously, the two worlds couldn't be realized at the same time. Again-------do I really need to go on? The point is that although God undoubtedly could have created a different system of nature, perhaps no system would have been without some negative consequences for humans . . . or without consequences worse than we presently have. Indeed, as I've just suggested, possibly the only way to get a system of nature with fewer negative consequences is to have more divine intervention.

M: I must say that the idea of a world without negative consequences for humans strikes me as nothing less than puerile. The preoccupation of the Western mind with suffering--the projection of some sort of hedonic paradise as an ideal is nothing but a provincialism of secular man. I know that you won't understand, H . . . and maybe neither will you, T--but suffering serves to heighten the value of oneness with the divine. The struggle, the struggle to rise above the senses, above suffering and pain--the struggle profoundly intensifies union with God. The union is simply more valuable because it is achieved within the context of suffering. What's more . . . union with the divine-------the bliss is so overwhelming that any sense of pain, sorrow, or suffering is simply blanked out.

H: Don't get carried away, M. Excuse me for saying so, but most of what you're saying strikes me as sheer religious rhetoric. Oh yes, I've read the mystics. I know what they say. All the same . . . .

M: I told you you'd never understand.

T: M, I agree with much of what you say. I accept your idea that pain and suffering simply get muffled--jammed out, if you will--during the encounter with God. I also accept your idea that struggle enhances the value of the encounter, as does suffering. . . . Yes, I think that these are valid ideas. The real question, though, the question we're focusing on, is whether we need as much suffering as we've got--particularly suffering for which humans are not responsible. A lot of the latter sort of suffering looks unnecessary. It's that suffering which I'm trying to account for to H.

H: With little success, I'll have to say.

M: Now be honest, H. T isn't doing so badly--given the system he's working with.

T: Thank you, M. At least I can count on the

objectivity of one person.

H: Objection!

T: Objection overruled! So . . . to continue-------
      actually, H, I wanted to go back to a point from
      our previous conversation. A basic difference be-
      tween you and me is over the extent to which God
      should intervene. You say that God should inter-
      vene more than he does now. I say, not so. One
      reason--the reason we talked about previously--
      is that more intervention is likely to be counter-
      productive. My point was that humans value their
      autonomy. What I emphasized was that they resent
      interference--I'd say, especially interference
      which smacks of ham-handed pressure. Vietnam gave
      us a fairly clear lesson about the effects of
      pressure. Our pressure on the north did little
      but intensify the resolve of the people to resist.

H: T, your precious autonomy issue is not going to
      get you anywhere. The commitment of human beings
      to autonomy is hardly anything to get excited
      about. Erich Fromm's Escape from Freedom and
      Sartre's writings on self-deception are forceful
      reminders that great segments of humanity want
      nothing to do with autonomy--it is to be eschewed
      like a cancer![4]

T: I'll agree that Fromm and Sartre were onto some-
      thing. . . . Perhaps what I need to say is that
      humans are ambivalent about their autonomy. One
      time they'll give it away as if it were going out
      of style; the next time they'll hang on to it like
      a bulldog. Actually, you might even find differ-
      ent reactions to autonomy at the same time. Look
      at Iran, for example. The people--the majority of
      them, as far as we can tell--have opted for a re-
      ligious authoritarianism. Yet at the same time
      they're hysterical about anything even bordering
      on outside interference. I mean, they see the CIA
      under every grain of sand. So what you have is
      the acceptance of a highly authoritarian govern-
      ment at the same time that you have the rejection
      of any outside interference whatsoever. . . . Now
      in the case of Iran the rejection of outside powers
      stems . . . to a considerable degree from past
      abuses; however, in other cases the rejection
      stems, I'd say, essentially from the desire for
      self-determination. Regardless of the propaganda

73

to the contrary, the modern movement of national-
ism cannot be written off simply to imperialistic
exploitation. Many colonies and territories were
governed in a relatively humane, enlightened, paternalistic manner--yet the impulse for indepen-
dence was not in the least diminished in these
colonies.

M: So what you're really saying is that even under a
divine paternalistic system, a system which was
paternalistic in the very best sense--even under
such a system humans would still tend to chafe, to
rebel. . . . I find that a reasonable enough view;
I mean, it's reasonable enough, given your concep-
tion of God. It's certainly the view of Biblical
literature. Regardless of how tough . . . or kind
God was to his people-------allegedly, they were
the object of his special care and attention. Yet
regardless of his care and attention, they usually
just shot out the lip.

T: Right. The point of the Bible seems to be that
humans have something of a territorial imperative.
What they really tend to say to God is: "Hey,
God, this is our territory. We may botch things,
but that's our business. We want to do things
our way!!"

H: Well now, if Frank Sinatra were here, he could
sing you a song. Of course, that wouldn't do
anything to improve your argument.

M: What's wrong with T's argument?

H: Something very obvious, I'd say. Natural evil was
designed to stimulate human freedom, you know.
It's a case of divine interference, then; and likely, as a result, to be counterproductive.

T: Not a bad objection, H; not bad at all.

H: Uh oh! I sense that one of your sophistic tricks
is on its way.

T: My good friend, you view me as a bottomless res-
ervoir of sophistic tricks. I assure you that at
best I am a shallow pond. . . . However, you will
allow me to defend myself, won't you?

H: Now just watch, M! See if I'm not right.

T: Well, I really wish I did have something tricky to say. All I can say, though, is-------I guess my point would be that natural evil is like a soft-sell rather than a hard-sell approach. Specifically, natural evil is not the result of any <u>special</u> activity on God's part, any obvious intru<u>sion</u>. As a result, it's less likely to inspire resentment or resistance than individually tailored instru-sions. Moreover, nature is regular . . . and thus can be controlled and adjusted to. In other words, it presents us with problems . . . we see as tractable.

H: So far, the old master of tricks isn't putting on much of a show.

T: It's the only show he's got, though. So . . . another thing I'd say is that nobody should have any resentment at all if the present system of nature puts no more pressure on us than any other system not incorporating constant divine interven-tion.

H: That's a pretty far-out possibility.

T: I can't say that it is or isn't--nor can you. Remember, until we specify systems in detail, we can't very well determine whether one possibility is far out, or another . . . "close-in." . . . At any rate, there's something else to consider. My view is that the reality of God, God's existence, can't be known. . . . I realize that you think otherwise, M, but . . . . . .

M: If you mean 'can't be known' in the Western sense of 'know', I fully agree. The reality of God is . . . experienced, not known in some rational sense. As the Upanishads say, "Other . . . is It than the known. And moreover above the unknown."[5]

H: Whatever the hell that means. . . . But please don't try to explain . . . because T hasn't finish-ed what he was saying. . . . As a matter of fact, his show is improving. He's saying something sen-sible now . . . about God's existence.

T: Thank you, my good friend. I'm glad you approve of what I said. We'll have to see, though, about what is yet to come. . . . As I said, God's exis-tence can't be known. That doesn't mean, of

course, the complete absence of reasons for believing in God. I'm convinced that we can come up
with reasons--damn good reasons, too; but not decisive reasons, not decisive by any stretch of the
imagination. Anyway, the implication for natural
evil is this: We can't very well resent natural
evil if we don't know that there's a god responsible for it.

H: Yeah, but what about the believer? Shouldn't he
      resent it?

T: Depends on the kind of believer he is. If he's a
      committed, trusting believer, he'll hardly get his
      back up over an attempt by God to affect man posi-
      tively. Or he may entertain the possibility I men-
      tioned earlier: No other system of nature would,
      apart from greater divine intervention, have fewer
      negative effects for man than our present system.
      . . . Or admitting that God's attempt to affect
      man through nature will raise some hackles, he may
      simply argue that the positive effects of the at-
      tempt far outweigh the negative. Take disease as
      an example. Man's response to it, his efforts to
      conquer it, has been one of the happy chapters in
      human history.

H: Words, words, words! Nothing but words! T, you
      underestimate yourself. You are definitely a re-
      servoir, not a shallow pond. However-------say, I
      just remembered a question. It's not exactly on
      the subject at hand . . . although . . . .

M: Oh, a privileged person, I see.

H: Well . . . the question really is on the subject--
      not natural evil . . . but on T's theodicy, gen-
      erally. The question came to me while I was in
      court the other day.

T: Then I guess it's out of the frying pan, into the
      fire for me.

H: This time, my fine-feathered friend, you better not
      be so cocky . . . because . . . . Well, here's my
      question. You go on and on about freedom, how it's
      a fundamental value, how it's worth the sacrifice
      of many other values, and so on and so forth. Yet,
      oddly enough, God isn't free--at least morally
      free. He's changelessly, necessarily good. My

question is how he's good at all, how he's even a
moral being. I thought you believed that the
freedom of indeterminacy is necessary for morality.

T: Unhappily, my good friend, your understanding of
my views is a bit deficient. I think we rule out
morality only when necessity comes from the outside in the form of . . . . Suppose that I give to
charity because somebody is holding a gun on me or
has kidnapped my child. In such a case the giving
doesn't count as a moral act--mainly because the
giving really isn't mine. I haven't been given a
choice, at least not much of one. It's almost as
if somebody picked my pockets. However, if the
necessity is from within, a necessity of intention
or desire, then obviously I am intending and acting . . . so that my action may be classed as moral.
. . . To simplify things, I guess I could just
say that we don't exclude an intention or action
from the realm of the moral just because it's
necessary. What we exclude from the realm of the
moral is the forced. An act which is forced is
just out as a moral act. Of course, I'll have to
clarify the term 'forced' further . . . .

H: Not now, please. Once you start, we might as well
forget about any other topic. . . . I gather, then,
that what you're saying is . . . .

T: Very simply, a being that necessarily intends and
does what is right is still a moral being. . . .
H, you don't believe that we have the freedom of
indeterminism, yet you certainly believe that we're
moral creatures. Right?

H: Right, but I thought you believed that nobody
could be moral apart from the freedom of indeterminacy.

T: No, a person who necessarily intends and does what
is right wouldn't receive my praise, but I'd surely
take pleasure in his intentions and actions, and
by all means call him morally good. So I definitely don't think the term 'good' is misapplied to
God, even though he necessarily intends and does
only what is right.

H: But now you're admitting that God isn't morally
free. He lacks your precious value of freedom--he

77

lacks a perfection.

M: Yes, T, how are you going to get out of that one?

T: Well, I hate to disappoint both of you, but I
    really don't see anything--or much of anything--
    that I have to get out of. As far as I'm concern-
    ed, you've handed me a non-problem. . . . Now
    don't mistake me--I'm grateful for your generosity;
    indeed, I only wish you both were . . . forever
    necessarily generous.

H: How is the problem I raised a non-problem? You
    can't win, you know, just by declaring victory.

T: If I only could! But please observe: If being
    indeterminately free is thought to be a perfec-
    tion, I'll simply deny that God has the perfec-
    tion. Just as not all possibles can be realized
    at the same time, so not all perfections can co-
    exist in the same being. If fixed moral goodness
    is a perfection, then God can't have it at the
    same time he has the perfection of moral freedom.
    Moreover, in the case of God constancy of charac-
    ter may be considered more valuable than moral
    freedom--for the very simple reason that God is
    omnipotent. In other words, I might argue that a
    moral freedom of indeterminacy is far too risky in
    an omnipotent being. Not, of course, that we have
    any control over God. God just is what he is.
    My point is that a moral freedom of indeterminacy
    might be considered a high value only in beings of
    limited power. . . . Now I could also take an en-
    tirely different course. Instead of denying moral
    freedom to God, I could admit it, saying simply
    that as a matter of fact God has, up to the pre-
    sent, been wholly good.

M: I prefer the course of saying that God is beyond
    morality. Neti, Neti.[6] Is God moral? No. Is
    God immoral? No. Human categories just don't
    fit.

T: With the result that God becomes a great blank, a
    Void--a term which is not uncommon for God in Eas-
    tern religion. My only question is, What does a
    person think of when he thinks of a void? If no
    human categories fit God, if no concepts apply,
    then what do you think when you think about God?

78

M: God, T, is a reality to be experienced, not thought about.

T: Rhetoric, M. You ought to be able to do better than that . . . or maybe you can't. Anyway, just look at what you said. You did use the word 'God', after all. Now did you have anything in mind, or didn't you? If your mind was a blank . . . then obviously you weren't thinking or saying anything at all. You may as well have yawned.

M: T, both you and M are so locked in to Western rationalism, Western logic chopping, that . . . .

T: If you mean that we think people ought to talk sense, you're absolutely correct.

H: I swear, you two are incorrigible. You get these off-the-subject attacks and just can't control them.

T: Oh, I thought you had gone to sleep.

H: No chance . . . so let's get back-------I want to go back to something you said earlier, T, about nature as a source of pressure . . . or as a stimulus. Even if I grant that nature puts pressure on us . . . .

T: Implicit in what I said was also the idea that nature as we have it--a nature which includes our bodies--this nature provides for a tighter disciplining of freedom than an arrangement in which nature is very forgiving . . . or, I might say, an arrangement in which we are not a part of nature-- we don't have a body. If we didn't have a body, our irresponsible behavior would present both God and other spirits with something of a problem. I mean, what could they do to bring us back into line?

H: Withdraw--cut off relationships.

T: Yes, they could do that . . . but withdrawal of fellowship is a limited means. A body introduces a whole range of means for affecting another.

H: That's just my point. If the world as we have it provides, as you say, for a tighter disciplining of freedom, then responsible freedom is being pitched on a low level, the level of rewards and punishments . . . or the level of natural consequences to action. . . . T and I have agreed, M --just so you know what we're talking about--we've agreed that God is aiming at the highest level of responsible freedom, the level where people do what is right just because it's right.

M: That makes sense.

T: When do you want my answer to your objection, H? If you give me . . . .

H: OK, now don't give me the mortal-blow line again. Just get on with what you have to say.

T: Oh, so you want to go the strictly-business route. OK, here we go. Point one: Possibly God tried a more restricted range of consequences. Maybe he went with pure spirits for a time--unsuccessfully.

H: Your proposal is strictly ad hoc.

T: Well, I will admit that I don't have a bundle of evidence--but then, I was only mentioning a possibility. I'd just remind you, though, that evidence for a world of spirit-beings would not be especially easy to come by. In fact, maybe a world of pure spirits isn't even possible--maybe there's no way to create one pure spirit different from another.[8] At any rate . . . point two: In order to minimize suffering, God may have gone immediately to a world which was as likely as any other to get some level of responsible freedom. You see, experimenting with other worlds, particularly worlds not too likely to succeed--experimenting with such worlds would have run the risk of additional suffering. Now as I said in our previous conversation, God might be willing to risk some additional suffering in order to get higher levels of responsible freedom. Yet when all things were considered, God may have decided against the risk and simply gone for a world as likely as any other to achieve some level of responsible freedom. I say that our world is such a world. . . . Point three . . . .

H: Say, am I going to be able to get a word in edgewise?

T: Strictly business, my friend, strictly business.
Point three: Our world is hardly a world which
locks people in to the lower levels of responsible
freedom. As I mentioned previously, the person who
takes natural consequences into account may very
well--may even be likely to--start thinking about
doing something just because it's right. In addi-
tion, our present world gives ample opportunity
to train people to focus on the rightness of action. Point four: A body increases the range of
freedom. You'll remember . . . .

H: Jesus, T, hold it. You're like a damned tank--
just keep rolling on. Now what do you mean, a
body increases freedom? I'd say it decreases
freedom. A pure spirit is without a whole range
of restrictions we have. Just take our spatial
limitations.

T: Yes, we are limited in terms of our movements . .
. yet maybe pure spirits are even more limited.
I mean, can a pure spirit move at all? The idea
of soul travel, out-of-body experiences, and so
forth--the idea may be popular these days, but
I'm not sure it makes any sense. However, even
if it does, pure spirits are still far more limited in their choices than we. Can they choose to
eat shrimp? or have sexual intercourse? or go
whitewater canoeing? or do any of the multitude of
things we do because we are physical beings in a
physical world? If God is after as much freedom
as he can get, if he wants us to have as broad a
range of choices as is consistent with getting us
to make responsible choices-------and naturally,
I say that this is what God is after. In fact,
I'd add freedom as another element in responsible
freedom--along with morality, rationality, and
autonomy. At any rate, my contention now is that
the body increases our range of choices.

H: But giving us disease--how rational was that?

T: H, you insist on ignoring the fact that we have a
system. Disease is one aspect of a total system,
a system which, as I said before, may present us
with no more difficulty than would any other system with no more divine intervention than our present system has.

H: And I told you, that's a far-out possibility.

81

M: And T told you that as long as you haven't pro-
     vided a detailed description of a world, you can't
     really say whether it is or isn't far-out. Be-
     sides, why say that God gives us disease? Much
     disease is directly attributable to our unbeliev-
     able eating and exercise habits, our lack of con-
     cern about hazardous wastes, our . . . . . .

H: M, I know all about that. We've already been over
     the human-stupidity route several times. I just
     don't see why disease is necessary--at least as
     much as we've got. God always seems to get car-
     ried away.

T: H, you're already ignoring what I just said: May-
     be no other system would give us fewer problems
     than we now have. Yet even if our world does pre-
     sent us with more difficulty than some other, I
     can maintain that any system with less difficulty
     would not be likely to stimulate responsible free-
     dom as much. . . . That's a view which seems to me
     to be as plausible as any you could come up with,
     my good friend.

H: I take it that on your view, T, we should stop try-
     ing to eliminate disease.

T: Stop trying to eliminate disease? What do you
     mean, H? What's your question have to do with any-
     thing I just said?

H: My question has to do with your whole justifica-
     tion of disease. You say that God created a world
     subject to disease. You also say that God doesn't
     do anything to eliminate disease--and shouldn't.
     Then you go on to say that God doesn't live by dif-
     ferent rules from us. Well, if that's so, why
     should we do anything to eliminate disease?

T: Now you're ignoring what I said when we talked pre-
     viously: The difference between us and God is one
     of roles, not rules. Remember, we talked about
     teachers and students? I could use other paral-
     lels--physicians and patients, for example. The
     point, though, is that God lives by the same rules
     --as we do. I'd say that the basic rule by which we
     should live may be generally stated in this way:
     We should aim at realizing the greatest net value
     possible in any situation.[9] As far as I'm concern-
     ed, the same rule holds for God.

H: Wait a minute, T. If God must try to get as much value as he can, then . . . then he must have been eternally creating persons . . . and the support systems for them.

T: Well, H, I think I could live with an eternally creating god . . . but I don't have to. My view is that the rule to try for the greatest net value possible applies to a situation of existing beings, not the situation of creation. In other words, God is under no obligation to create; but once he decides to create, he must aim at realizing the greatest net value possible.[10]

M: On this matter of creation I'd definitely have to side with H. What possible reason would there be for not creating eternally? Why should God all of a sudden decide-------of course, the idea that God decides is, after all, terribly primitive. Yet I guess I have to remember that we're dealing with your anthropomorphic god, T.

T: M, you have this lovely penchant for pejorative labels . . . for applying pejorative labels to views you disagree with. I hope you realize that I could indulge myself similarly. Naturally, I'm going to follow the dictates of the great chariot-eer, reason, and not indulge myself.

H: Naturally! However, you are indulging yourself in some fanciful views about creation.

T: Well, am I? I think the closest human parallel to creating is . . . parenting. Suppose, then, that a couple would, by having children, add value to the world. Are they under obligation to have children simply because the children would add value to the world? Not at all, as far as I'm concerned.

H: Do you mean that if the children would be the means of resolving the problem of the arms race, the parents wouldn't be under obligation to bring them into the world?

T: No, that's not what I mean. You're talking about a different kind of case. I'm not supposing that the children would solve any problems. I'm merely supposing that the children would be additional centers of value . . . and thus would introduce

additional value to the world--apart from solving
any social or world problems. Isn't your view
that God should eternally create persons just because persons, being valuable in themselves, would
add value to the universe?

H: Well yes; that's what I had in mind.

T: All right, that's what I thought. . . . Of course,
I might add that-------I could very well maintain
that persons, bare persons who haven't done or experienced anything yet, have no value. Value
comes with human choice and experience . . . so
that a person may end up introducing net negative
value to the universe. The value-balance for
Hitler, for example, was strongly tilted in the
negative direction. Now obviously, if the chances
that persons will introduce net-value cannot be
stated--no rational projection may be made--or the
chances are just fifty-fifty, God would certainly
not be under any obligation to create persons.

M: T, you're wrong about persons, dead wrong! The
self, the true Self, is infinitely valuable in itself. Admittedly, most people live only at the
level of the surface, the phenomenal, self, the
self of which we're conscious from moment to moment. They never realize what they truly are. As
the Upanishads say, "That thou art."[11] Yes . . .
our true Self is of infinite value.

T: I'm afraid, M, that you and I would not soon agree
on the notion of the true self.

H: Nor would I . . . so let's get back to the main
issue.

T: You see, M, H has not relaxed his rigid monitoring
of this discussion one little bit.

M: No . . . at least not for me. . . . However, I have
no objections to getting back to the main topic.
Actually, I'm here just as a . . . novice, just a
novice, ready to learn from you more experienced
types.

H: Yes, T and I are clearly journeymen in this business of religious and philosophical discussion.

M: You're partly right . . . but you were saying, T

-------as I remember, you were talking about rules and roles. The difference between our obligations and God's is one of roles, not rules.

T: Right. Assuming that the rule is to seek the greatest net-value possible-------that's a defensible rule, anyway; it's as plausible as any other rule or set of rules. So, assuming that the rule holds for God as well as for us, I say that any difference in specific obligations between God and us is attributable to a difference in roles. Let me be more specific. I say that a world in which free selves act responsibly is better than any other kind of world. The question, then, is: What is the best way for God to get responsible freedom? I say, a hands-off policy--a relative hands-off policy. The same question, though, goes for mankind: What course of action on our part is most likely to bring about responsible freedom? I say in this case, the first step is for each person to be responsible himself, for each person to bring responsibility into the world in the one area over which he has the greatest control. That's fundamental. After we've done a job on ourselves, then maybe we can get concerned about making others responsible. . . . Now in the case of others, what I'd point out is that in some of our attempts to make others responsible we resort to means which make them very uncomfortable . . . or which do nothing in the short term to relieve suffering. Just take AA again. As we know, the people in AA won't even begin to fool with somebody who they don't think is serious. They'll let him hit bottom. In fact . . . .

H: As you said, T, we know all about AA.

M: But a reminder doesn't hurt.

H: M, you're supposed to be listening. Remember, you're a novice.

M: Yes, I know . . . but listening to you almost made me forget.

H: Touché......All right, T, finish what you were saying . . . and wipe that grin off your face.

T: Oh, my apologies for not being suitably grave . . . . . But if you wish me to continue-------I know a

psychiatrist who simply won't touch a patient unless the patient is really hurting, is really
feeling anxiety. He says that the patient who
isn't hurting is unlikely to stay in therapy--you
know, out of sight, out of mind . . . with the result that nothing ever gets solved. So a psychiatrist may very well not attempt to bring immediate
relief to a patient's anxiety. Indeed, a psychiatrist may even try to induce more anxiety--or perhaps I should say, he may follow procedures which
he knows will only heighten the patient's immediate anxiety. . . . In the same way, God, whom we
could view as the divine psychiatrist-------my
apologies to you, M. I know how offensive . . . .
. . .

M: No, you have no idea . . . although I have to ad-
    mit that I'm becoming hardened to your crass re-
    presentations of the deity.

T: Psychiatrists would be offended by your remark----
    ---but to continue. Now I'm coming back, H, to
    your question about disease.

H: Well really, I'd given up on that. I just assumed
    that your thinking was--as you said, out of sight,
    out of mind.

T: I admit that the issue has been out of sight . . .
    for a while, but not out of mind--my mind. Get-
    ting back to disease, then, I'd say-------here's
    what I could say. God, the divine psychiatrist,
    employs disease, among other things, in his ef-
    forts to bring humans to responsible freedom. Now
    admittedly, a patient in therapy looks for the im-
    mediate relief of anxiety . . . and he will do
    everything and anything to reduce it--except, per-
    haps, look at his real problem. The therapist,
    on the other hand, may take the posture of benign
    neglect, or, as I said, may even try to increase
    anxiety. Naturally, the therapist is also ultima-
    tely after the reduction of anxiety--but only as
    the consequence of getting at what he views as the
    root of the difficulty. . . . The point, then, is
    -------really, there are two points: Just as a
    psychiatrist sometimes employs anxiety to accom-
    plish his purposes, so God has employed disease
    and other natural phenomena to accomplish his pur-
    pose of getting responsible freedom; and just as
    a patient's approach to anxiety does not parallel

86

the psychiatrist's, so our approach to disease does not parallel God's.

H: Your analogy doesn't go, T. A patient should have the same approach to anxiety that the psychiatrist does.

T: If you don't like the analogy, we could go back to the teacher-student analogy. The teacher is after critical thinking--the student should be after the same. In order to achieve critical thinking the teacher introduces problems--that's one means he employs to stimulate critical thought. Naturally, he doesn't turn around and solve the problems he's introduced--that's the student's responsibility. Here we clearly have two different roles, with the same overall objective. . . . But we have an identical situation in the psychiatrist-patient relationship. Yes . . . I still think my psychiatrist-patient analogy holds. The psychiatrist is after mental health; the patient should be, too. The psychiatrist may introduce anxiety as a means of ultimately achieving mental health . . . but nobody would say that a patient should induce or maintain anxiety in himself. That would be absurd. The patient's job is to resolve his anxiety--resolve it by getting to work on his underlying problem. . . . In the case of God . . . God is after responsible freedom. We should be, too. One means that God uses to get us going on the path of responsible freedom is disease. Disease is a problem which God has given us to solve. The problem is of such a nature that-------in working to solve the problem, in seeking to reduce or eliminate disease, we're really working on our underlying problem of becoming responsible . . . because working on disease is a very important way of being responsible.

M: T, if I may just break in for a moment-------will that be permissible, H?

H: Sure, be my guest.

M: Well, T, we've taken great strides toward the elimination of disease. Already smallpox has been eliminated world-wide, and in the developed nations a whole list of diseases has, for all practical purposes, been eliminated--polio, diphtheria, whooping cough, and so on and on. What happens,

then, when disease is totally eliminated? . . .
Oh, we might have some new brands crop us, but .
. . . . . .

T: No problem, M. I never said that God's experiment
has to last forever. As a matter of fact, an un-
ending experiment would be a little strange--not
one I'd like to try to square with God's goodness.

H: Hey, are you saying what I think you are? Are you
saying that the elimination--or virtual elimina-
tion--of natural evil will bring a halt to God's
grand experiment?

T: Almost. I don't think God would have to wait for
us to cope with every form of natural evil. Just
coping with disease ought to do the trick; God
ought to get the message from that alone. If responsibility still remains at the starting gate
after disease has been conquered, then God has ex-
pended one of his best shots--God has used one of
his most powerful stimuli--without effect. Nothing else is likely to do any better.

H: Well, I'll say this for you, T: You're the first
person I know of who's ever put something of an
empirical test on a theodicy. However much I may
grade-down your theodicy, I'll at least have to
give it points for having definite empirical consequences. I mean, at least it's not one of these
religious positions which is true no matter what
may occur. . . . But tell me, what happens if God
calls off his experiment? What then?

T: He goes to a world as good as any he can get.

H: You mean a heavenly world?

T: Well, maybe a heavenly world . . . but surely a
world with much less freedom than we now have.

H: Yes, that would seem to follow. . . . But let's
not speculate about the kind of world God might
go for . . . because I want to get back to disease.
Suppose that disease is everything you say it is,
a first-rate challenge and stimulus to be responsible. Why--pray tell--why does the stimulus have
to be so overwhelming? Why not start on a lower
level? In fact, the question goes for natural
evil generally--why not less pressure to begin

with? If more pressure is needed, then put it on.
In other words, why not turn the screws slowly?

M: H, I'm afraid you have run out of ammunition. T
has already answered your question several times
over. Turning the screws slowly would require al-
tering nature in some way--a rather clear sign of
the divine. Apparently, you're not taking T's ambiguity argument very seriously.

T: I told you, H, you were going to be surprised at
the mileage I'd get out of my ambiguity argument.
. . . But there's another point, a point raised
by your figure of turning the screws slowly. That
figure brings to mind--at least to my mind--the
Vietnam conflict. Our policy there of turning the
screws slowly was about as bankrupt as any policy
could be. The policy might be equally bankrupt in
the case of getting responsible freedom. If God
is trying to minimize suffering in his experiment,
then he'll have to go with the combination of factors which is most likely to succeed. What might
work best with us--what might do the job--is fairly heavy pressure all at once. You see, light
pressure might be something like a vaccination.
You get just enough of a disease--really, an altered form of the disease--just enough to build up
immunity. God naturally didn't want us building
up immunity, so he hit us hard and fast to begin
with. . . . I guess to sum it all up, I'm main-
taining-------what it really comes down to is that
God has chosen the optimum arrangement for achieving responsible freedom. I'd not claim that this
view is unquestionably true, only that it's . . .
. . . .

H: as plausible as its denial. I memorized the refrain long ago. . . . Jesus, what can I do to get
through to you?

T: I guess you and I ask ourselves similar questions.

H: OK, T, let's forget about disease. Let's talk
about death. There's no death in a heavenly state
. . . so why do we need it here? What's so great
about it?

M: Part of your problem, H, is that you just can't
seem to think outside of your Western orientation.
Neither can you, T, for that matter. The basic

89

problem with the Western mind is that it views death as some sort of unmitigated disaster. Yet death is no disaster. It's a transition, a transition to another level of existence.

H: You bet--sometimes a much lower level. So death may not be as super as you make out, M.

M: I don't think of transition to a lower form of existence as a disaster. It's the working out of one's _karma_, and will, in the end, bring about the movement of the soul to higher forms of existence.

T: Naturally, M, I'm not in the least averse to viewing death as a transition. That is certainly the view within Christianity.

H: Yeah, but you ought to be averse. If our earthly existence is so fine, as you say it is, then why change for another form of existence?

T: I don't think I ever said that our earthly existence is "so fine"--as you put it. In fact, I said just the opposite: Things haven't been going too well. All that I've maintained is that our earthly existence is compatible with the total goodness of God. . . . So what I might say is . . . . I might say that death provides a limit to our participation in God's experiment. Also, you have to realize that if death were to be eliminated, our present natural order would also have to be eliminated--unless, of course, God intervened continuously to sustain life. Another consideration is this: Death is an especially valuable test of freedom. If a person will not act responsibly under the constraint of death--when the very existence of himself or another is at issue--he's hardly likely to act responsibly under a lesser constraint. And finally, I'd point out that death puts pressure on us to get our act together, to avoid dallying, to make our contribution to responsible freedom straightway. Nobody knows that he will have another crack at life. He may be-lieve in an afterlife, but he certainly doesn't know that there is one. In fact, the most he should say is that belief in an afterlife is plausible.

H: That's hardly what most people say, though. And what's worse, those who are most convinced usually opt out of any attempts to improve things down

90

here. You know, "This world is not my home."
That mentality.

M: Speaking of home, I must take leave of you gentle-
men. Have to pick up my husband in ten minutes. .
. But the conversation has been enjoyable--some-
thing of a welcome break from the usual here.
We'll have to continue another time.

H: It'll be a little hard, at least for T. He's leaving you all-------I don't mean he's checking out
for good; you know . . . making the transition to
the afterlife. What I mean is, he's quit, given
up the ivory-tower life for the hard, cruel free-
enterprise life.

M: You're not serious.

T: I haven't quit. I'm just taking a two-year leave.

M: Well, I declare! I'll have to hear more about
this . . . but not now. I've got to run. Joe is
a fanatic about being on time . . . and I'm already
going to be late. . . . Nice to have met you, H.

H: Same here, M.

T: We'll get together. I'll be dropping by every now
and then. Wouldn't miss the lounge conversation,
you know.

M: Yes, we all know about that. . . . See you later
. . . .

NOTES

[1]Karma may be viewed as the cosmic law of justice, the moral
law of cause and effect whereby one's present state of existence
is the exact consequence of the sum of one's conduct during his
past states of existence. The law is generally viewed as strictly
impersonal, not dependent in the least on a personal god's meting
out rewards and punishments. The ultimate aim of the religious
pilgrimage is moksha or release--release from the cosmic law of
karma through the realization of one's true self or Atman, a state
which is nothing less than identity with the Ultimate (God, that
is, Brahan).

[2] Plato, _Republic_, in _Great Books_, pp. 388-89 (Book VII: 514-17).

[3] See on this point Bruce Reinchenbach, "Natural Evil and Natural Laws: A Theodicy for Natural Evils," _Inter. Phil. Quart._, 16 (1976), 194-95.

[4] Jean-Paul Sartre, _Being and Nothingness_, trans. Hazel E. Barnes (New York: Philosophical Library, Inc., 1956), Part I, chap. 2.

[5] Sarvepalli Radhakrishnan and Charles A. Moore, _A Source Book in Indian Philosophy_ (Princeton: Princeton University Press, 1957), p. 42.

[6] Neti, Neti means literally 'not this, not this'. The terms are meant to emphasize the indescribability of God or Brahman.

[7] See Richard Swinburne, "Natural Evil," _Amer. Phil. Quart._, 15 (1978), 295-301.

[8] On the problem of identifying more than one purely spiritual being see Terence Penelhum, _Religion and Rationality_ (New York: Random House, 1971), pp. 154-61.

[9] The view here is not some straightforward form of utilitarianism. Among other things, moral values are given special status and are not thought to be dependent on a utilitarian justification. For example, the good will is thought to have value independently of its effects; truthfulness has value beyond the positive consequences of being truthful; and so forth.

[10] See Jan Narveson, "Utilitarianism and New Generations," _Mind_, 76 (1967), 62-72.

[11] Radhakrishnan and Moore, _Source Book_, pp. 38, 69.

PART IV: ANIMAL SUFFERING

H: T, I've got to say that your yard captures the
    prize on this block--a veritable riot of color.
    Roses, callas . . . .

T: No, those are cannas.

H: Oh, Callas, cannas . . . whatever. Your pansies
    are my favorites. They're blooming kind of late
    this year, aren't they?

T; Yes, the cool spring prolonged their life. . . .
    What's up?

H: Oh, I just came by to check a rumor.

T: You mean you heard that I was trying to sell the
    Purple Cow.

H: Well, I knew things had been tough, but . . . . .
     . .

T: That's hardly the word for it. Either we sell--
    at a loss, naturally--or we go bankrupt in another
    couple of months.

H: That bad, huh? Hell, man, you were doing a great
    business last summer. What happened?

T: You tell me. About mid-November everything came
    to a screeching halt. We've been eating up our
    savings for a number of months now . . . and we're
    about down to scraps.

H: You going back to the university?

T: I really wanted to start a landscape-gardening
    business. As you know, I had one in grad school--
    made more than most of my profs. But my damn leg
    is still giving me some trouble. . . . . . . Phaedo,
    how the hell did you get out? Down! Down, dammit,
    you stupid dog.

H: God, that dog's become a monster. . . . Go on
    pooch, beat it! . . . I thought the dog belonged
    to your daughter.

T: Yeah, it does . . . technically. She just doesn't

keep it. She was supposed to rent a house with a
yard but couldn't find anything but an apartment.
So guess who has become the de facto owner? Come
here, Phaedo. Get in there. . . . Stay, dammit!
OK, good dog. . . . . . Now maybe we can have
a little peace.

H: Your dog reminds me of something.

T: What?

H: Well, maybe you're not in the mood for heavy conversation.

T: My good friend, when have I ever not been in the
mood for heavy conversation? . . . Do you remember
that unbelievably boring New Year's Eve party we
got sucked into--when was it, three years ago?

H: Christ, man, how could I forget? Hell, we got
there at 9:30 and were ready to leave at ten. Our
conversation was the only thing that made the even-
ing half-way tolerable.

T: As it was, you and your wife cut out at 12:30.
Slightly obvious.

H: Hell, I'm getting too old to torture myself just
to keep somebody else happy. Besides, you're no
one to talk. You left a half-hour later.

T: Yeah, my wife concocted this beautiful story about
having to get up early to go fishing with our old-
er daughter and her boy friend. . . . I went fishing with them just to keep my wife honest . . .
and to avoid all the New Year's Day television. .
. . At any rate, I take it that you want to take
another whack at my theodicy.

H: Well, it has been our constant topic for about a
year now.

T: Yes, and neither one of us has convinced the other.
Either we're both pig-headed . . . or both our
positions are equally plausible . . . or . . . . .
. .

H: Maybe only one of us is pig-headed.

T: Yeah, I thought you might say that. Anyway, what's

94

on your mind?

H: You know, one thing we've neglected to talk about
    --don't ask me how--but I've been thinking about
    it recently; I mean, animal suffering.

T: Oh, afraid I can't offer you much on that issue.
    I've been going back and forth on it for some time
    myself. In fact, maybe we ought to discuss some-
    thing else. I'm afraid you've raised the issue
    just to embarrass me.

H: I know, you're terribly afraid . . . Socrates!

T: I see you're in a complimentary mood. For your
    compliment I shall permit you a question.

H: Apparently you're not in a very generous mood . .
    . but I guess I better take whatever I can get.
    OK . . . here's what I want to ask. You know how
    much you make of God's restraint in employing mir-
    acle. Your whole ambiguity argument is what I have
    in mind. Well, I don't see how the argument will
    help in the case of animals--I mean, for the period
    prior to when man entered the world scene, whenever
    that may have been. Granted that now God would
    have to intervene regularly to reduce animal suf-
    fering; but in pre-history-------why not just an
    entirely different nature, a nature in which the
    lamb lies down with the lion? In fact, why a pre-
    history at all?

T: My friend, you must be preoccupied with other mat-
    ters. Surely, you can see that if men and animals
    had been created at essentially the same time--as
    Biblical literalists say was the case--if the lit-
    eralists are correct, or if a switch in the course
    of nature occurred at the time man entered the
    scene-------either way ambiguity would have been
    reduced drastically.

H: Yeah . . . yeah, I guess you're right. My question
    wasn't the sharpest, was it? . . . Well, I suppose
    that what I really have in mind-------I just think
    you're putting far too much weight on the prop of
    ambiguity.

T: And you are begging the question with your word
    'prop' . . . . Yet perhaps I am putting too much
    weight on ambiguity. You certainly should have

95

gathered by now that I'm far from happy with several parts of my theodicy. Of course, long ago I give up on flawless, watertight solutions to complicated metaphysical problems.

H: OK, but there comes a time when explanations start getting fixed up so much--they get so strained that they appear to be nothing but rationalizations.

T: Granted, but I don't thing my theodicy is at that point--yet. If and when it gets there, I hope I'll be among the first to abandon it. I've abandoned other philosophical positions before, you know. . . . However, for now, I'm still sticking with my theodicy. . . . As for ambiguity, it's not the only line of defense I have.

H: Well, then, let me hear of another line.

T: OK, I'll just remind you of something. I'll remind you that animal suffering is hardly on the same level as human suffering.

H: Jesus, T, that line of defense isn't any better than your ambiguity line. I mean, if you're going to talk about animal suffering-------hell, how provincial can you be? You'd hardly get any agreement from animals!

T: Absolutely. I wouldn't get any agreement from animals . . . because they can neither agree nor disagree. That's just my point. Animals are not on the same level as humans. Among other things, they don't have the foresight . . . and certainly not the self-consciousness of humans--which means that animals don't have half the problems with suffering that humans do. Foresight and self-consciousness do nothing but exacerbate suffering. In fact, cut foresight and self-consciousness and you've cut a considerable amount of human suffering in the way of anxiety, guilt, and fear. Remember Epicurus' statement that the fear of death, along with the fear of the gods--these two fears are at the root of human misery?

H: Only vaguely. Can't say that I've read any history of philosophy recently. But I agree with what he said.

T: OK, but in the case of animals I venture to say
      that the fear of death is, if not totally absent,
      barely present. As for the fear of the gods . . .
      well, I don't know anyone who's claiming that ani-
      mals have even the rudiments of religion. . . .
      No, H, given our understanding of animals--and per-
      haps we're off base--but given our understanding,
      we have to conclude that an enormous amount of
      suffering present on the human level is just not
      present elsewhere in the animal kingdom. That's
      not a provincial view--at least no more so than
      any of our other best attempts to arrive at an ob-
      jective understanding of animals.

H: T, you're just kicking up a great cloud of sophistic
      dust. All that you just said has little to do with
      the real issue, which is needless animal suffering.

T: Well, we ought at least to be clear about the na-
      ture and extent of animal suffering. We undoubted-
      ly have a serious problem, but perhaps not quite
      as serious as we first imagined. . . . However, let
      me take another crack at the problem. Let's look
      at it from the standpoint of the function of pain.
      . . . Now pain is clearly something we try to
      avoid; all the same, pain is essential for making
      our way through this world. Just think of those
      people who have deficient pain systems. Special
      provisions have to be made for them so that they
      will not harm or destroy themselves. I recall
      reading a while back about a leper village in
      India. Leprosy, as you know, often destroys the
      nerves in the various parts of the body affected.
      Well--the story is really kind of gruesome--this
      Indian village was plagued with rats, which would
      come in at night, while the people were sleeping,
      and gnaw on their hands or feet, without the peo-
      ple having the slightest idea that anything was
      happening.

H: Jesus Christ!

T: I said it was kind of gruesome. . . . Anyway I
      read about the situation in a magazine article
      which was making an appeal for cats. The group
      making the appeal--some kind of religious group,
      as I remember--well, the group wanted to send cats
      to the leper village in order to take care of the
      rats. Never heard of the outcome--whether the
      rats or the cats won.

H: You've got a morbid sense of humor . . . but I get
     your point. Sure, I agree that pain is . . . kind
     of like-------I guess it's sort of our radar sys-
     tem. However, you're assuming the present course
     of nature. Why not a system in which the body
     would immediately restore itself whenever it was
     damaged?

T: My friend, we've already been over that. Remember
     . . . nature is a system. The scenario you sug-
     gest may not be possible within any consistent
     framework of laws . . . or the framework in which
     it is possible may have defects far worse than our
     present system . . . or the system may be possible
     --or I should say, your scenario may be possible
     only with . . . . . .

H: more divine intervention--gotcha! . . . So far,
     we're not getting very far with the issue of ani-
     mal suffering, are we? Maybe I can come at the
     issue from another angle. . . . How about death
     in the animal world?

T: How about it? It's no more on the level of human
     death than is animal suffering on the level of
     human suffering. In fact, I'd say that death in
     the animal world is only marginally evil at worst.

H: I still think animals ought to have a vote on this
     point.

T: Regardless of my profound commitment to civil
     rights, I fear that in this case-------look, H,
     let's suppose that death is a termination for ani-
     mals--it ends everything, kaput! Now a major rea-
     son why death has sting for humans is that it ends
     relationships. In the case of animals, I'd say
     that the sting is reduced to little more than a
     pin-prick.

H: I wouldn't discount relationships on the animal
     level. Some animals even exhibit mourning behavior
     when another animal dies. I remember reading some-
     where about the mourning ritual of South African
     baboons. When one of their members dies, they hud-
     dle together at the time of the setting of the sun,
     fix their eyes on the Western sky, remain silent
     for a time, and then start making sounds, sounds
     which they make only at the time of death or sep-
     aration.

T: Oh, I'm as aware as anyone else of the sense of loss that an animal can exhibit. Yet generally speaking, you'd surely admit that animal relationships lack the depth of human relationships, with the result that any break is more easily adjusted to. As a matter of fact, just across the board, animals lack the depth of humans--or to be more exact, I guess I should say, animals lack the potential for growth and development that is found in humans. As an example, take my dog . . . my daughter's dog. The dog eats, chases squirrels, fetches balls, sleeps--that's about it. Her range of interests is extremely limited, with the consequence that her life is largely repetitive. Sure, maybe she could chase a rabbit rather than a squirrel . . . but how different would that be? And what's more, she has no taste for the finer things--those open-ended pleasures, like the pleasures of art and beauty. The dog just sniffs our Degas reproduction . . . and never have I seen her remain fixed before a sunrise or sunset. In other words, the capacities of my dog, along with other animals, are extremely limited; but limited capacities mean limited growth. Death, then, is not an interruption of an open-ended process of growth-- or what I should say is, a process which can be an open-ended process of growth. You and I are aware that some people never rise much above the animal level.

H: I more than you, my friend. I really get some low life coming through my office. Anybody who believes in inborn moral rules just hasn't been around.

T: No, H, a person could believe in inborn or innate rules. All he'd have to do is say that the rules had become obscured or suppressed--sort of like the Biblical idea of a seared conscience. In any case, the notion of morality offers us one way to point up the differences between us and other animals, the differences relating to growth and development. Moral perfection is an ideal for us; that is, it's certainly an ideal we can have . . . but not one animals can have; at least, I assume that the capactities of animals do not meet the minimal requirements for moral action and motivation. Humans, then, can have the ideal of moral perfection, whereas animals cannot. By 'ideal' I mean a goal of the nature of a mathematical limit; it's approached but never reached. In other words, humans have a goal which, in effect, requires an eternity to pursue.

H: OK . . . suppose that for now I go along with your argument that animal death doesn't interrupt an open-ended growth process. I still have the problem of broken relationships, as well as the problem of suffering, to throw at you.

T: I don't think I'll even bother to duck . . . because you're throwing nothing more than marshmallows. . . . First of all, on relationships-------let's get serious, H. Animals are put in zoos, shifted from one zoo to another, from one mate to another. . . . Remember the great panda caper at the Washington zoo?

H: That had to be one of the funniest events in recent history. Brought over the male from the London zoo because of the inept male at the Washington zoo. I mean, talk about hilarious. The old London male was just as inept as ours. A real national comedy--slightly symbolic, I'd say, of the bureaucracy, of Washington itself.

T: Right . . . but don't forget my point: The animals were shifted around according to the latest bright idea of the zoo officials. The same is done with animals in pet shops, not to mention cattle -------need I continue?

H: Well . . . .

T: No question--we, the majority of us, don't seem to bother a whole lot about animal relationships. So I suggest that you find another soap box, my friend--only don't try the pain and suffering one. We've already talked about pain as . . . as a radar system--your terminology, as I remember. We've also talked about nature as a system--how maybe the overall assets of our present system outweigh those of any other system. . . . Of course, I could suppose a system with animals alone, no humans--a system in which there was less suffering for animals than in our present system. Yet if God had started with the system . . . . . .

H: So it's back to ambiguity again. . . . OK, just let me ask you: How the hell long is ambiguity supposed to last? Doesn't it ever get cleared up?

Isn't the Christian view of the afterlife that
ambiguity gets removed? St. Paul certainly talks
about knowing then as he is known now.[1] But if
ambiguity gets reduced in the afterlife, why not
now?

T: Well, first of all, did I ever say that ambiguity
      never gets reduced now? Perhaps I need to back-
      track a little and talk about the function of am-
      biguity. Actually, I'd say that ambiguity has
      several functions. In our previous conversations
      I think I've stressed the adventure function: Am-
      biguity makes religion an adventure rather than a
      cake-walk. But ambiguity also has other functions.
      Two I'd mention are a testing function and a sti-
      mulus function.

H: You better explain.

T: By 'testing function' I mean this: Ambiguity is a
      test of a person's seriousness about the pursuit
      of truth. As for the stimulus function, what I'd
      say on that score is really assumed in what I just
      said about the testing function: An ambiguous
      situation should stimulate a person to try to un-
      derstand.

H: I see . . . and you would maintain that the at-
      tempt to understand--to understand in the area of
      religion--the attempt normally bears some fruit.

T: Right. I'm no Kierkegaard--at least as I under-
      stand Kierkegaard. I don't hold that the person
      of faith constantly treads the precipice of un-
      certainly, no matter how many leaps of faith he
      has taken. The religious pilgrim--the adventurer--
      normally makes some discoveries, brushes against
      the divine.

H: You talking about religious experience?

T: Yes . . . essentially. You see, another value of
      ambiguity is that it steers us away from the outer
      to the inner. In other words, I say that the
      search for God must be basically a search of in-
      ner, or spiritual space. Ambiguity--the ambiguity
      in the external world--turns us to the world of
      the spirit.

H: You said, though, as I remember, that the inner

world does not dispel ambiguity.

T: My point was that as of now substantial ambiguity
    remains. However, if ambiguity is to be reduced,
    the inner world offers more hope than the outer.
    What I mean is that the reality of God, if it is
    ever to be apprehended, cannot be apprehended
    through any external sign.

H: Apparently, you're forgetting your ideas about
    miracles. You believe, as I remember, that mir-
    acles could be arranged in such a way as to practi-
    cally dispel doubt. I think you mentioned--yes,
    you suggested an Elijah-like demonstration every
    few years.

T: Right . . . yet even so, the inner world still re-
    mains the choice locale for apprehending God as
    personal. Nowhere else can we come to as pene-
    trating an understanding of the divine personhood,
    of the divine Self.

H: I'm not sure that inner space is the best place to
    apprehend anything. I'm not in the least impress-
    ed with arguments from religious experience. I
    think that too many other ways to explain reli-
    gious experience are available.

T: Other explanations there are--granted; but I'm
    with James in saying that the hypothesis of a di-
    vine Other is the most credible hypothesis . . .
    a damn good hypothesis.[2] You see, H, the people
    reporting encounters with the divine are not all
    weirdos, kooks, fanatics, or freaks. Many are as
    sober and sophisticated in their thinking as you
    or I ever thought of being. They are perfectly
    aware of naturalistic explanations; they simply
    don't think the explanations will wash. I met a
    clinical psychologist just last month-------he
    was the main speaker at that religious meeting
    they had . . . where was it? the Sheraton?

H: Right. Now there was a weird bunch if I ever saw
    one.

T: They were different, all right--different, I mean,
    from the routine in religion; but maybe that's
    all to the good. In any case, this clinical psy-
    chologist had been "grabbed and shaken by God."
    Those were his words.

102

H: You really don't mind where you're seen, do you?

T: Well, if you're looking for oil, you go wherever
    it might be found, whatever the environment may be.
    And you're not embarrassed if you come up with a
    dry hole. . . . But getting back to my story--this
    psychologist kept saying over and over, his con-
    stant refrain about his experience was, "I just
    can't explain it." So here's a guy, far more
    self-conscious than most people, far more aware
    of what makes him tick-------he'd been through
    analysis, as I remember. Anyway, here's a sophis-
    ticated, critical guy who all of a sudden has a
    religious experience. I mean, my good friend,
    what if you--sort of out of the blue--had a reli-
    gious experience?

H: Yeah . . . that'd sure make the headlines. Don't
    hold your breath, though.

T: Don't forget: This psychologist wasn't expecting
    anything any more than you are. That's why he
    couldn't figure out his experience--not in terms
    of any naturalistic theory. Obviously, some aca-
    demician who's never met him, who doesn't know him
    in his concreteness, may brush him off, with knee-
    jerk quickness, into some neat little explanatory
    category. Obscurantism, you know, is hardly passé
    in the so-called intellectual community.

H: I'm not sure how to respond to that one . . .
    since I don't buy supernatural explanations of
    religious experience.

T: I'm talking about reflex responses--tossing some-
    thing off without seriously considering it. . . .
    Anyway, my main point is that religious experience
    is one way of reducing ambiguity. Yet there's
    another point here: Ambiguity gets reduced in re-
    ligious experience--it gets reduced essentially
    because of a growing sense of the divine or be-
    cause of repeated encounters with the divine.
    What I'm driving at is that the sense of divine
    presence--union with God--well . . . it's essen-
    tially what religion is all about . . . and it's
    the reason why we have to go to inner space. You
    see, even if the outer world furnished us with
    clincher arguments for a divine reality, we'd
    still have to take the inner route, the route
    leading to divine encounter. As things stand,

we're forced to the inner route from the very
start--or should be--because of the weakness of
arguments from the external world. At least I
think the arguments are weak.

H: I'm with you on that one . . . although, as I
said, I'm not as sanguine as you about arguments
from religious experience. However, I don't want
to argue about the matter. Let's get back to the
main issue . . . to animal suffering. You've been
saying that a different natural order prior to the
coming of man would clearly indicate divine acti-
vity--I mean, the switch from the one order to the
other would indicate divine activity. But why an
entirely different order? Why not the same natural order as now but constant divine intervention
--constant miracle--to eliminate animal suffering?
How would anyone ever know that the miracles took
place? Naturally, if we didn't know about the
miracles, we'd have no problem on the score of ambiguity.

T: And naturally, you'd not have raised any objection
to my theodicy. I'm not in the least averse to
constant miracle--as long as nobody knows anything
about it. In fact--and this is the main point--if
you can't show that God didn't do precisely what
you say he should have done, your objection simply evaporates. . . . As I said, my good friend,
you must be preoccupied . . . or you're just losing your touch.

H: Yeah, my objection wasn't anything to write home
about, was it? You can forget that one. . . .
But T, tell me now, just why couldn't God at least
have shortened up the pre-history of life some--I
mean, make it 100 million years rather than three
and one-half billion years plus? A little less
suffering, I'd say.

T: H, we're on to reruns again. I really can't say
any more than I've already said. Nature is a system, so that any change such as you suggest would
undoubtedly mean massive system-wide change, the
results of which we simply don't know. A speedier
evolutionary process might just involve greater
human suffering, less incentive to be responsible--
I can't say. I've admitted mystery on this point

long ago, but it's a mystery which you share with me because you're no better off than I when it comes to knowing the effects--or even the possibility--of a radically changed nature.

H: Well, then, what it gets down to is . . . I don't see how the search for God even begins to justify all the animal suffering prior to man.

T: I think your problem is that you won't let yourself admit the superiority of human values.

H: Here you go again.

T: Yes . . . but not in a way peculiar to me. Our whole way of life--which I haven't seen you abandoning lately--our whole way of life assumes the superiority of human values. Just take the steak you ate last night.

H: I didn't have steak.

T: Well, you probably wished you had. The fact is that you eat steak--with the greatest of pleasure. So . . . for your hedonistic satisfaction you are willing to have cattle slaughtered. Now if that's justifiable--you and I seem to assume that it is-- if it is, then clearly we're viewing human values as incomparably higher than animal values. But surely, if hedonic values justify the slaughter of animals, the values associated with the search for God certainly justify animal suffering prior to man. One claim seems no wilder to me than the other.

H: Slaughtering animals, as you put it, doesn't involve pain.

T: You've got to be kidding, H. We're talking about snuffing out life, animal life. . . . Besides, I hardly think you or I can definitely say that all pain is absent from the final stroke. The animals are not anaesthetized, and the procedure is surely not 100% effective--I mean, we can't forget Murphy's Law! And . . . just consider the whole process of bringing an animal to slaughter. Hardly a pleasure tour, I'd say. You think that cattle plan their whole life around traveling in a semi-trailer or railroad cattle-car? It's not their trip to Mecca, you know. . . . Actually, instead of referring to steak, I guess I should have mentioned the duck and geese you eat. Your renown as a hunter is the focus of considerable conversation in the local honkytonks. The point, naturally, is that people generally don't get excited about the cruelty and suffering associated with hunting . . . or fishing. So, unless you're willing to jettison the value assumptions associated with our treatment of animals, I don't think you can raise the slightest objection to my contention that the value of ambiguity in the human situation outweighs the disvalue of animal suffering during and prior to the time of man.

H: OK, let's admit for now that my penchant for hunting and for eating steak is a flaw on an otherwise impeccable moral surface. Let's suppose that I'm a vegetarian on moral grounds. I won't touch animal life; I won't do anything which risks the suffering of animals--I mean, needless suffering, just for my pleasure.

T: Before you get too carried away with your new lifestyle, I'd just remind you that animals--mice, any number of rodents, nutria, birds, you name them--animals generally, can become real pests, destroying, chewing to pieces, dirtying-up, and so on. Now how are you going to justify our elimination of pests?

H: I guess I'll appeal to health grounds . . . the same grounds I'll use, by the way, to justify our use of animals in experimentation--something you apparently forgot to mention.

T: No, I just didn't want to unload too much on you at once. . . . But now, just note: For a healthy lifestyle we wipe out huge animal populations. Does that tell you anything about our values? Besides, we often eradicate animals for strictly aesthetic reasons. I mean, why do we get after gophers and moles? Essentially because they ruin a good carpet of grass. . . . No, my good friend, if you're going to take animal life seriously, you're going to have to alter your lifestyle radically. Yes, and if you do, you better be ready to take a lot of flak.

H: OK, let's suppose that I've radically altered my lifestyle, and that I'm taking all sorts of flak.

T: In that case I couldn't be as persuasive with you as I now can. Naturally, I'd look for inconsistencies in your lifestyle. However, if you were fairly consistent, then . . . I guess I'd be reduced simply to pitting my value judgment against yours. Not the happiest situation I can imagine . . . although again I remind you that my task is not to convince you of the correctness of my value judgment--only that it's as plausible as yours.

H: All this "as-plausible-as-yours" business seems to me to be a tacit admission that value judgments lack objectivity.

T: Not necessarily--although I'll just remind you of something I said a long time ago: My theodicy doesn't require the acceptance of moral objectivity.

H: Hmmmmm, I forgot that. Wouldn't be much of a Christian theodicy, I'd say.

T: Undoubtedly, not to some . . . but to others . . . .

H: Well, I see that we have another topic for our future conversations. However, right now, let's get back to ambiguity. I've got one more question --I mean, one more for the present moment. Actually, it's a question we never finished up on--about the afterlife. Remember, we were talking about St. Paul's statement that he will know in the afterlife as he is known now?

T: Right.

H: OK, if ambiguity is so great, how come it gets cleared up--bam! just like that?

T: I don't interpret Paul to be saying that perfect knowledge is attained instantly upon entering the afterlife. He may very well be talking about the results of a long process; or put differently, he may be representing the afterlife in terms of its possibilities, not its actuality at the moment one enters it. The idea of instantaneous fulfillment is one I reject out of hand. The idea fits well, I suppose, in our present culture of instant everything: instant foods, all packaged and ready to go--just stick them in the microwave. . . .

Speaking of food, though, I've got some excellent split pea soup I made yesterday. How about some? Personally, I'm famished.

H: Any homemade bread?

T: Right.   Wheat bread.

H: You're on!

NOTES

[1] 1 Corinthians 13:12.

[2] William James, The Varieties of Religious Experience (New York: The Modern Library, 1902), Lecture XX and Postscript.

INDEX

ad hoc, hypothesis of previous
worlds as, 80
Adler, 35
afterlife
belief in, 90; and removal
of ambiguity, 100-101
ambiguity
and a change in natural
order, 88-89, 95; elimination in afterlife, 107;
functions of, 101; and history prior to man, 95; reduction or termination of,
100-101; and reduction of
natural evil, 63; its role
in religion, 50; and the
search for God, 101-102;
and the search for know-
ledge, 52-53, 68, 101; and
Whitman-type cases, 51-54
animals
capacities of, 96-97; death
of, 98-100; relationships,
98-100
animal suffering, Part IV
compared to human, 96-97;
and search for God, 105-107
atemporality of God, as explanation of knowledge of
future, 7-9, 20
autonomy
and Iran, 73-74; and resistance to interference or
pressure, 44-45, 73-74, 76;
and responsible freedom,
42-43

benevolence
alleged requirements of, 3;
and hands-off policy, 52;
in heaven, 11
body
increases range of freedom,
81; and the tighter dis-
ciplining of freedom, 79

cave, parable of, 68
Christian
theodicy, special problems
of, xii-xiii; view of God's
intervention, 46
clairvoyance, and rational
projection in God, 13
consistency defense, ix
creation
conditions for, 3-4, 14, 15;
of this world, an experiment,
9-10, 60; conditions for calling off the experiment, 15,
17, 18, 87-88; and God's
knowledge, 6; must God eternally create, 83-84? of necessarily responsible persons
impossible, 25-27; and net-
value principle, 14; and
Pangloss Principle, 3-4; and
P_1, 4; and P_2, 6; and responsible freedom, 10, 41-43,
80-81; and unwarranted risk,
15-16; value requirements of,
4-14
crucial statement in theodicy, xi

death
reasons for, 89; of animals
vs. human, 98-100
deductive nature of explanation
in theodicy, xi
depravity of man as part of
free-will defense, 25
determinism, 29 (f. 3)
disease
and different roles of man
and God, 82-87; and distribution of natural evil, 67-
69; as part of a total system, 81; positive response
of man to, 76; a stimulus to
seek knowledge and responsible freedom, 67-68, 87;
total elimination of, effects
on God's experiment, 87-88

109

distribution of natural evil,
non-selective, 66–70

empirical test of theodicy,
87–88
Epicurus on fear of death and
gods, 96
eternal creation, 83–84
evil (see natural and moral
evil)
natural, 30 (f. 11); moral,
30 (f. 11); as necessary
for good, 24; no problem of
in case of impersonal god,
60
experiment
creation of world as, 9–10,
60; conditions for starting,
14; conditions for calling
off, 11, 15–18, 87–88; freedom as justifying risks of,
13; need not achieve perfect
responsible freedom, 25; and
suffering, 60; trial and error, 10, 24; why not called
off, 17–18?
explanation
nature of in theodicy, ix–
xiii; tentative super-
natural in case of mystery,
46–48

faith, rational, xiv
finitude, human, and God's
hands-off policy, 54
foreknowledge, divine
impossible in case of in-
determinate events, 7, 9,
19; problems of eliminated
in theodicy of this book,
23; if unlimited, why not
create only responsible
persons, 23–27?
freedom (see also responsible
freedom)
and a body, 81; and God's
aim, 81; incompatible with
necessarily responsible

freedom (cont'd)
person, 25–27; of indeterminism and God's perfection,
78; relation to morality,
77–78; value of, 13
free-will
consistency defense, ix;
defense, 10–11; and the depravity of man, 25; theodicy,
ix
Fromm, Erich, on freedom, 73

God
his atemporality, problems
of, 8–9; as ground of knowing the future, 7–9, 20
benevolence, alleged re-
quirements of for God, 3,
11; and a hands-off policy,
52
of Bible, temporal nature
of, 8
experience or encounter with
(see religious experience),
50, 63–64, 72, 102–103; as
basic aim of religion, 103–
104
his hands-off policy (see
hands-off policy)
not indeterminately free,
76–78
his knowledge: cannot know
the indeterminate, 7–9, 19;
knows man and his condi-
tions, 14; is omniscient,
6–7; can make rational projections of future, 12–13;
must have data to go on, 13–
14, 69–70
knowledge of: God as beyond
categories of knowledge, 78;
existence cannot be known,
75, but good reasons may be
given, 76
as impersonal, and conse-
quences for problem of evil,
60
intervention of, man's resistance to, 44–45, 73

T's Principle, 21

value
  of ambiguity as justifying
  animal suffering, 105–107;
  balance, 15; net-value
  principle in creation, 14;
  objectivity, 16, 107--not
  guaranteed, xi–xii; of persons and the necessity to
  create, 83–84; requirements
  in creation, 4, 14–15; superiority of human to animal,
  105–107; statements, nature
  of good reasons for, xi–xii
Vietnam and the resistance to
  pressure, 73
void--God as void, 78–79

Whitehead on religion as an
  adventure, 50
Whitman and Whitman-type
  cases, 34, 51
  and ambiguity, 52; and
  conditions for God's intervention, 52–54
world, present
  as best of all possible, 3;
  an experiment, 9; as good
  as any alternative for getting responsible freedom,
  80, 89, 98; some other world
  may be better than world as
  it has been, 3, 11, 90
world of responsible freedom as
  best, 10, 16, 85
worlds prior to this, 14, 80
worlds--other: whether
  really possible depends on
  detailed description of,
  75, 82